Take your learning f
this book's online c

All the titles in Kogan Page's Creating Success series have individual *CPD-accredited* online courses to help you develop your business and workplace skills.

Quick and easy-to-use: 1-hour courses
to develop your skills quickly

CPD accreditation: Each course awards
CPD points and certification for tangible
proof of your achievement

Additional resources: Downloadable resources
will reinforce what you learn

Bespoke packages: Discounted corporate
and bespoke offers are also available

Free preview: Module preview to confirm
you are picking the right one

Find out more about the course for this book at
koganpageonline.com

Save 25%
on all courses using the code CREATINGSUCCESS

CREATING SUCCESS
SERIES

The above titles are available from all good bookshops.

For further information on these and other Kogan Page titles, or to order online, visit **www.koganpage.com**.

Dealing with Difficult People

Fast, effective strategies for handling problem people

Roy Lilley

KoganPage

First published in Great Britain and the United States in 2008 by Kogan Page Limited
Fourth edition 2019

2nd Floor, 45 Gee Street	122 W 27th St, 10th Floor	4737/23 Ansari Road
London	New York, NY 10001	Daryaganj
EC1V 3RS	USA	New Delhi 110002
United Kingdom		India
www.koganpage.com		

© Roy Lilley, 2008, 2013, 2016, 2019

The right of Roy Lilley to be identified as the author of this work has been asserted by him in accordance with the Copyright, Designs and Patents Act 1988.

ISBNs

Hardback	978 0 7494 9879 5
Paperback	978 0 7494 8641 9
Ebook	978 0 7494 8642 6

British Library Cataloguing-in-Publication Data

A CIP record for this book is available from the British Library.

Library of Congress Cataloging-in-Publication Data

Names: Lilley, Roy C., author.
Title: Dealing with difficult people : fast, effective strategies for handling problem people / Roy Lilley.
Description: 4th Edition. | New York : Kogan Page Ltd, [2019] | Series: Creating success | Revised edition of the author's Dealing with difficult people, 2016. | Includes bibliographical references.
Identifiers: LCCN 2019004933 (print) | LCCN 2019010953 (ebook) | ISBN 9780749486426 (Ebook) | ISBN 9780749486419 (pbk.) | ISBN 9780749498795 (hardback)
Subjects: LCSH: Psychology, Industrial. | Interpersonal conflict. | Problem employees.
Classification: LCC HF5548.8 (ebook) | LCC HF5548.8 .L493 2019 (print) | DDC 650.1/3–dc23
LC record available at https://lccn.loc.gov/2019004933

Typeset by Hong Kong FIVE Workshop
Print production managed by Jellyfish
Printed and bound by CPI Group (UK) Ltd, Croydon CR0 4YY

CONTENTS

ABOUT THIS BOOK

This is not a book to be read from cover to cover. It is not *War and Peace*, although with a bit of luck it will give you some ideas on how to have more peace than war.

It is a book to dip into, look for the character or situation you're having problems with, find a solution, apply it and move on. Life is too short to spend it having a row with people.

This is a book to scribble on the pages, rip bits out and do all the things with that your old school would give you detention for! This is a source book but not a reference book. A book to dive into but not to get immersed in.

This is a book you can use to improve your own performance or use as a source of ideas to work in groups to improve the performance of your team.

To the uninitiated, difficult people can be the bane of your life, a blot on your landscape and a real pain to work with. This book is designed to help you to enjoy difficult people. Once you have the key, you can unlock them, influence them, get them working for you, and they'll never notice.

The first rule

There is no such thing as a difficult person. There are just people we need to learn how to deal with.

The second rule

Re-read the first rule.

01
A short course in human relations

This book is all about dealing with difficult people. Get it? Not difficult situations or difficult issues. It's the people we are focusing on. Certainly difficult people will give you a bad time, horrible situations and awkward issues to overcome. However, at the centre of it all are the people. By understanding people, how they tick, what they think and why they act like they do, we can avoid the bad times and horrible situations, and overcome the awkward issues.

If we plant some seeds and the flowers don't bloom – it's no good blaming the flower. It may be the soil, the fertilizer, not enough water? Who knows? We just find out what the problem is and fix it.

If we have difficulties with our families, the people we work with or our friends, what's the point of blaming them? Figure out the reason and then fix it.

Difficult, who me?

Yes, you! Before you can think about dealing with difficult people, let's start with you. Are you difficult? Are you the one out of step? Are you the one with the problem? Try the exercise below. Do you think these are the kind of things difficult people tend to say? Probably not. This exercise should help you to evaluate yourself and consider honestly if you could be the one with the problem after all.

Exercise

Keep a tally chart, for how many times you can use the phrases below in one week:

Tally
I admit I made a mistake
You did a good job
What is your opinion?
Would you mind?
Thank you

Reflect on the impact these phrases had on your interactions with others.

Tip

Really difficult people are most likely to be selfish and inwardly focused. They won't give a toss about you. For them, it's all about them. So, don't let them get under your skin. So the number one rule in dealing with difficult people is: Don't take it personally!

OK, so what do you do, when facing an encounter with a difficult person? Easy. Before you enter an encounter with a difficult person, prepare. You can do this by following the thought process outlined in Figure 1.1.

Figure 1.1   Preparing for an encounter with a difficult person

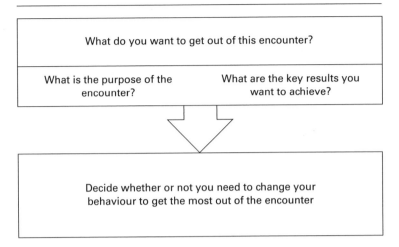

This doesn't mean you have to let rude people trample all over you. But it does mean you don't get into a bare-knuckle fight.

Exercise

Next time someone is rude to you, try this: *'I'm not sure quite what you meant by that remark. Can you explain it to me please?'* It usually means they will tone down. As they calm down, don't forget the 'please'!

Here's some bad news for you: nice people are not always like you! Yes, yes, I know the world would be a much simpler place if everyone was like you, but they're not. They will have different backgrounds, different education, different perspectives and different ambitions. They will be motivated differently and think differently. And they can still be nice people!

Think about it! The brutal truth is they don't care about you. This may come as something of a shock, but there aren't too many people out there who care too much about you. There's your mother, she probably still loves you; family, partners and a few friends, maybe. But, when push comes to shove, you're on your own.

How we treat each other is largely a product of how we feel about each other. Most folk start off neutral, some downright antagonistic, but the fact is most people couldn't care less about you.

It gets worse! Difficult people don't care about you at all. They care about themselves. They are into them, in a big way. That's why they're difficult.

What can you do about it? The brutal answer is not much! It is very unlikely that you will change them. Why bother? There is a much easier way.

Remember this: Difficult people are predictable people. Avoid having a row. If you can, don't argue. Settle a dispute by looking for a higher authority that is neutral. A rule book, systems protocol, service manual or company policy may provide the answer. Don't get personal.

That simple fact makes your life much easier. How many times have you heard folk say, '*Oh, don't bother with him, he's a misery.*' Or, '*Don't ask her, she finds fault in everything.*'

You see, difficult people are not just difficult with you. They are into themselves and are, usually, difficult with everyone.

Tip

Predictable is easy. You can prepare for difficult people, you can plan for them, you can plot, scheme and collude against them. They are stuck in their ways. All you have to do is manoeuvre.

This doesn't mean becoming a soft touch, or a pushover. It means you use your brains more than your emotions. The trick is to decide in advance what you want out of an encounter, plan accordingly and go for it. Table 1.1 shows some approaches you might want to consider.

Table 1.1 Approaches to dealing with difficult people

Difficulty	Approach	Example
If you know someone is a nit-picker and a stickler for detail?	Give them detail.	In the report, I've included all the background I can think of, including spreadsheets for four scenarios. Let me know if there's something else you need.
If someone is abrupt...	Get straight to the point, avoid flannel and go to the heart of the matter.	I know you are very busy, so I'll come straight to the point. What do you think about this next phase of the development?
If someone is an egomaniac...	Tell them how good they are.	Jane, I know you are the neighbourhood expert on this, so I've put the detail together and made a couple of recommendations. But can I leave it to you to come up with some alternative directions, if you think they might be better?

The strategy is easy. You won't change a difficult person by being difficult. They don't care about you, they care about themselves. By deciding what you want out of the encounter and being prepared to manoeuvre, trim, sidestep, change, call it what you like, you end up winning. You end up getting what you want.

It's so easy that you will end up wishing everyone was difficult – because the difficult ones are easiest to manage!

Summary points

- The first thing that will help you understand how to deal with difficult people is the fact that we are all different – and that can be a good thing! But ultimately, people are all in it for themselves; it's not about you.

- Don't forget to consider if you are being difficult! Be honest with yourself about this.

- Take the time to prepare for an encounter with a difficult person.

- Once you've decided what your goal for the encounter with someone difficult is, you can tailor your approach to them and manoeuvre around anything.

02
The seven classic difficult types

(or how to sound like an expert in the time it takes to drink a cup of coffee)

Too busy to read the whole book right now? That's fine, take a break and read these next few pages – it's all you need for now. You'll be an expert!

Recognize anyone?

There are seven basic personality types that get filed in the difficult tray. Elsewhere in this book I deal with many more types, but they are derivatives of the seven deadly sinners. Here's the quick guide to becoming an expert complete with expert views from some leading thinkers for you to draw upon.

Table 2.1 Seven personality types

Type 1 Hostile, aggressive, belligerent and offensive

How can YOU recognize them?

Frightening, alarming and downright terrifying. They are often bullies and control freaks. We are going to look at three main personality types for this category:

- The Sherman tank
- The sniper
- The exploder

The expert view

- *The Sherman tank*
  They come out charging. They are abusive, abrupt, intimidating, and overwhelming. They attack individual behaviours and personal characteristics. They bombard you with unrelenting criticisms and arguments. Sherman tanks usually achieve their short-run objectives, but at the cost of lost friendships, and long-term erosions of relationships.

- *The sniper*
  Snipers prefer a more covered approach. They put up a front of friendliness behind which they attack with pot shots, use innuendoes, non-playful teasing and not so subtle digs. Snipers use social constraints to create a protected place from which to strike out at objects of anger or envy. They pair their verbal missiles with non-verbal signals of playfulness and friendship. This creates a situation where any retaliation back at the sniper can be seen as an aggressive act, like you are doing the attacking not the defending. Much like the Sherman tank, snipers believe that making others look bad makes them look good. They also have a strong sense of what others should be doing, but their constant cutting remarks usually de-motivate colleagues rather than producing results.

- *The exploder*
  These tantrums can erupt out of conversations and discussions that seem to start friendly. Usually these tantrums occur when the exploder feels physically or psychologically threatened. In most cases an exploder's response to a threatening remark is first anger followed by either blaming or suspicion.

SOURCE Bramson (1988)

| Type 2 |
| Complainers, grouches and the sourpusses |

How can you recognize them?

Complainers moan like hell about everything but never seem to take any action to change anything. It is almost as if they like having something to moan about. Complainers are not the individuals who have legitimate complaints and a desire to find a solution to the problem. The complainer is someone who finds fault in everything. Sometimes they do have a real complaint, but rarely do they want to find a way to fix the problem.

The expert view

The constant complaints can cause people around the complainer to feel defensive. Complainers view themselves as powerless, prescriptive, and perfect. These beliefs cause complainers to convert useful problem solving into complaining. Their feeling of powerlessness causes them to think that they cannot change things so they had better complain to people who can. Their prescriptive attitude gives them a strong sense for how things ought to be and any deviation from that produces complaints. Complaints are a way for the complainer to confirm that they are not in control or responsible for things that are done wrong, reaffirming perfectionism.

SOURCE   Bramson (1988)

Tip

Given that moaners and groaners have a strong sense of how things should be, could you harness their energy to enable them to change things to how they ought to be? It is important to take on board the idea that just because someone has certain character traits they are not necessarily a write-off.

Type 3
The silent, unresponsive and quiet ones

How can you recognize them?

A silent, unresponsive person deals with any disagreeable situation by shutting down. Ask them what they think and you'll be rewarded with a grunt!

The expert view

The unresponsive use silence as their defensive weapon, to avoid revealing themselves, so they can avoid reprimand. On the other hand it can be used as an aggressive, offensive device as a way to hurt you by denying access. An unresponsive person in some cases might be distrusting of others, which explains their need to clam up. Sometimes, keeping the silence is used as a way to avoid one's own reality. When words are spoken, they reveal thoughts or fears of the thinker, which can be frightening. It can be used to mask fear, sullen anger, or it can be a spiteful refusal to co-operate. This type of person can be maddeningly difficult to deal with because of the communication barrier they put up. In most cases, this person will not be very willing to converse openly. When they speak, there might be prolonged periods of silence due to a lack of confidence in themselves and their lives. This can result in a breakdown of communication, which leads to an unproductive interaction. Those who portray this type of behaviour usually display such body language as staring, glaring, frowning, or folded arms in an uncomfortable position.

SOURCE   Lewis-Ford (1993)

Tip

Dealing with difficult people is about just that – dealing with them and using the talents they do have. Good management is about getting the best out of everyone.

Type 4
The super agreeable

How can you recognize them?

The super agreeable is always reasonable, sincere and supportive to your face but doesn't always deliver as promised. They want to be friends with everyone, love the attention. However, there's a darker side. They tend to lead you on with deceptive hints and references to problems that have been raised, and will willingly agree to your plans of accomplishing the task at hand, only to let you down by not delivering.

The expert view

Everyone needs to feel acceptance and to be liked by others. There is a balance point that integrates our needs to do a job well and to find a reasonable place in the pecking order with a reasonable concern for being liked. For this type of person, the burden is so far to one extreme that they feel an almost desperate need to be liked by everybody. Their method of gaining acceptance is to tell you things that are satisfying to hear. They also use humour as a way to ease their conversations with others. This type of difficult person presents a problem when they lead you to think that they are in agreement with your plans only to let you down. Their strong need to give and receive friendship can conflict with the negative aspects of reality. Rather than directly losing friendships or approval, they will commit themselves to actions on which they cannot or will not follow through.

SOURCE Bramson (1988)

Tip

Relationships, alliances – the workplace cannot function without super-agreeable people. A good manager recognizes staff who take on more than they can deliver. To deny them a piece of work is, in their eyes, to deny them friendship. To snub them. There is a fine balance to be considered. Feelings can be easily damaged. Reality is often the very cold antidote to the warmth of friendship.

Type 5 The negativist

How can you recognize them?

The negative person is a corrosive influence on groups and can be very demotivating for the individual. Buried in all this negativity is the capacity for a 'deep personal conviction' and the ability to see through tasks where they have direct control. Everyone has something to offer. Can you live with the thought that there are no bad staff, just poorly performing managers?

The expert view

The negativist is best described as a personality that not only disagrees with any cumulative suggestions in a group situation, but also is the first to criticize group progress. While their criticism could be interpreted as constructive, this disrupts progress in a work environment and could negatively impact interpersonal relationships within a working situation. Another common reference to the negativist is the sceptic. Like the negativist these individuals like to tear apart and shoot holes in whatever is being said at the moment. They wear out their welcome over time as people catch on to their chronic negativity. Inside the character of a person who is considered to be negative is a person who is having difficulties dealing with a deep seated inner conflict. This usually comes from a feeling that they don't have power over their own lives. The negativist is unable to work through basic human disappointment. A negativist believes that everyone can relate to and understand the well of disappointment they feel towards humanity and our own imperfection. While these people are so incredibly embittered about life and how it treats them, they are capable of having deep personal convictions about any task that is placed in front of them. However, if they are not in direct control of the project, it will fail because they believe that no one can handle or perform a task quite like they can.

SOURCE Rosner (2000)

Type 6
The know-all

How can you recognize them?

Know-alls have an overwhelming need to be recognized for their intellectual ability. They are bores, dull and very tedious! Know-alls are very complex people. They can be bullies. They appear so certain they are right, it seems pointless to argue. They can be very persuasive. They like to communicate as if they are talking to a child. Very annoying! The second know-all type dominates conversations and likes being the centre of attention. The problem is if they read press cuttings on a subject, they are an expert. Some know-alls are not above making up for any information or knowledge deficit by inventing a few facts.

The expert view

The know-all could be suffering from lack of self-importance or may be unable to participate at the level in which he/she would like to contribute to the group's idea pool. Taking the time to listen to a know-all's endless speeches could lead to loss of time in completing projects or assignments. Know-alls' problems stem from a need for others to think of them as being important and respected. Usually people who are confronted with a situation involving a know-all are faced with a frustration. This usually leads to tension in work relationships.

SOURCE   Raffenstein (2000)

Tip

Is there a role for a know-all? If they like the power of knowledge, maybe the answer is to make them an expert. Send them on a course.

Type 7 **The indecisive, the ditherer, the hesitant**

How can you recognize them?

Inside the indecisive is a perfectionist trying to get out. They just can't seem to manage it. According to Bramson, this type of personality usually comes in two types. One wants things done their way or no way; the second is someone who, at times, intentionally drags out discussions by injecting different viewpoints, frustrating everyone in the process.

The expert view

The indecisive person may be one who usually is not good at communicating their own thoughts, needs, and opinions to those around them. At best these people stall because they are unable to cope with stress at a high and low level. In order to deal with the stress they procrastinate, which brings down co-workers and other people around them. At best they stall by not considering alternative ways of getting a job done. So those on the receiving end of the indecision lose enthusiasm and commitment to the project or person which eventually brings down the team. Despite their success in evading the decision, the typical indecisive gets stressed over a various amount of tension. This doesn't mean that they don't communicate a decision or feeling through indirect communications. In fact, they are masters in body language, low moans or grunts, or even eye contact. If the indecisive chooses to verbally make contact with other people it comes out in short phrases or sentences. Many times, these pieces of information get either ignored or shoved aside by co-workers who are already frustrated by the lack of communication they have received from that person. They are also sensitive and might withhold information because they are worried about how it will be perceived by a group or person they are communicating it to. If the information is not sensitive they feel that their opinions don't matter and that someone else will deal with a conflict or problem that they are worried about.

SOURCE   Bramson (1988)

Exercise

Think back to some times when you have encountered difficult people. Tick off the kinds of difficult people you think you have encountered. Now rate their level of difficulty, with 1 being the ones you found least difficult. This should tell you the kind of difficult people you need to work harder at being able to deal with.

Type	Encountered?	How difficult?
Hostile, aggressive, belligerent and offensive		
Complainers, grouches and sourpusses		
Silent, unresponsive and quiet ones		
The super agreeable		
The negativist		
The know-all		
The indecisive, the ditherer, the hesitant		

First, the diagnosis

What type are they? Brad McRae, author of *Negotiating and Influencing Skills: The art of creating and claiming value*, suggests four steps to accurately diagnose someone:

- The first thing to do is to watch and take notice if you've seen this behaviour in three situations with this person. The reason for this is because the first two times are probably chance but by the third time it's probably a pattern.

- The second thing to do is notice whether or not this person is dealing with a lot of stress. Stress may be causing this adverse behaviour and is not a regular occurrence.

- The third thing to do is to ask yourself if you've been suffering from any exceptional stress. Stress on you may be causing you to see the world in a way that is contrary to what is actually going on.

- The fourth: have you had an adult-to-adult conversation with this person? There are times when the other person may or may not know that their behaviour is causing a problem for you and talking to them can clear up what turns out to be a simple misunderstanding.

McRae tells us, 'The reason people get into difficult situations with difficult people is because they allow themselves to become emotionally hooked. Often, the more we try to break free of these situations the more ensnared we become until some of us crack.'

Why do we get hooked or sucked in by difficult people? Back to McRae: all people have a set of values or beliefs that guides their behaviour throughout life and especially in encounters with other people. Each individual's set of values is unique to them.

Here is McRae's list of 15 of the most common core beliefs:

- I must be loved or accepted by everyone.
- I must be perfect in all I do.
- All the people with whom I work or live must be perfect.
- I can have little control over what happens to me.
- It is easier to avoid facing difficulties and responsibilities than to deal with them.
- Disagreement and conflict should be avoided at all costs.
- People, including me, do not change.
- Some people are always good; others always bad.

- The world should be perfect, and it is terrible and catastrophic when it is not.

- People are fragile and need to be protected from the truth.

- Others exist to make me happy, and I cannot be happy unless others make me happy.

- Crises are invariably destructive, and no good can come from them.

- Somewhere there is the perfect job, the perfect solution, the perfect partner and so on, and all I need to do is search for them.

- I should not have problems. If I do, it indicates I am incompetent.

- There is one and only one way of seeing any situation, the *true way*.

Exercise

Look at McRae's list of core beliefs. Decide which core value, or values, you most relate to. Now think of a time when you had to deal with a difficult situation. Does this help you to see why you found the situation challenging? Understanding leads to controlling yourself and your emotions better.

Tip

According to McRae, if we learn the first step, to control ourselves, then we have a better chance to control others and the situations we find ourselves in.

Robert Bramson, author of *Coping with Difficult People*, lists tips for each of the seven types we will come across. Here is his 'at a glance guide'.

The type	The response
The hostile Sherman tank	• Give them a little time to run down. • Don't worry about being polite; get in any way you can. • Get their attention, perhaps by calling them by name or sitting or standing deliberately. • Getting them to sit down is a good idea. • Maintain eye contact. State your own opinions forcefully. • Don't argue with what the other person is saying or try to cut them down. • Be ready to be friendly.
The hostile sniper	• Smoke them out. Don't let social convention stop you. • Provide them with an alternative to a direct contest. • Don't focus on their point of view, be sure to involve everybody. • Do move fast to try to solve any problems that arise. • Prevent sniping by setting up regular problem-solving meetings. • If you are a witness to a situation with a sniper, stay out of it, but insist that it stop in front of you.
The hostile exploder	• Give them time to run down on their own. • If they don't run down, cut into the tantrum with a neutral phrase such as 'Stop!' • Show them that you take them seriously. • If possible, take a breather with them to the side and in private.

The type	The response
The complainer	• Listen attentively to their complaints even if you feel guilty or impatient. • Acknowledge what they are saying by paraphrasing their statements and checking out how you feel about it. • Don't agree or apologize for their allegation even if, at the moment, you don't accept it as true. • Avoid the accusation–defence–re-accusation ping-pong argument. • State and acknowledge facts without comment. • Try to move to a problem-solving mode by asking specific, information questions, assigning limited fact-finding tasks, or asking for the complaints in writing, but be serious and supportive about it. • If all else fails, ask the complainer, 'How do you want this discussion to end?'
The silent and the unresponsive	• Rather than trying to interpret what the silence means, get them to open up. • Ask open-ended questions. • Wait as calmly as you can for a response. • Use counselling questions to help move them along. • Do not fill in the silence with your conversation. • Plan enough time to allow you to wait with composure. • Get agreement on or state clearly how much time is set aside for your 'conversation'. • If you get no response, comment on what's happening. End your comment with an open-ended question. • Again, wait as long as you can, then comment on what's happening and wait again. Try to keep control of the interaction by dealing matter-of-factly with 'Can I go now?' and 'I don't know' responses.

The type	The response
	• When they finally open up, be attentive and watch your impulse to gush. Flow with tangential comments. They may lead you to something relevant and important. If they don't, state your own need to return to the original topic.
	• If they stay closed, avoid a polite ending, terminate the meeting yourself and set up another appointment. At length, inform them what you intend to do, since a discussion has not occurred.
The super agreeable	• You must work hard to surface the underlying facts and issues that prevent the super agreeable from taking action.
	• Let them know that you value them as people by telling them directly, asking or remarking about family, hobbies, wearing apparel. Do this only if you mean it, at least a little!
	• Ask them to tell you those things that might interfere with your good relationship.
	• Ask them to talk about any aspect of your product, service or self that is not as good as the best.
	• Be ready to compromise and negotiate if open conflict is in the wind.
	• Listen to their humour. There may be hidden messages in those quips or teasing remarks.

The type	The response
The negativist	• Be alert to the potential, in yourself and in others in your group, for being dragged down into despair. • Make optimistic but realistic statements about past successes in solving similar problems. • Don't try to argue them out of their pessimism. • Do not offer solution-alternatives yourself until the problem has been thoroughly discussed and you know what you are dealing with. • When an alternative is being seriously considered, quickly raise the question yourself of negative events that might occur if the alternative were implemented. • At length, be ready to take action on your own. Announce your plans to do this without equivocation. • Beware of eliciting negativist's responses from highly analytical people by asking them to act before they feel ready.
The know-all	• Make sure you have done a thorough job of preparing yourself; carefully review all pertinent materials and check them for accuracy. • Listen carefully and paraphrase back the main points of the proposals, thus avoiding over-explanation. • Avoid dogmatic statements. • To disagree be tentative, yet don't equivocate; use the questioning form to raise problems. • Ask extensional questions to assist in the re-examination of plans. • As a last resort, choose to subordinate yourself to avoid static and perhaps to build a relationship of equality in the future.

The type	The response
	Where the know-all is not threatening or bullying:
	• State facts or alternative opinions as descriptively as possible and as your own perceptions of reality.
	• Provide a means for them to save face.
	• Be ready to fill a conversation gap yourself.
	• If possible, cope with them when they are alone.
The indecisive	• Make it easy for the indecisive to tell you about conflicts or reservations that prevent the decision.
	• Listen for indirect words, hesitations and omissions that may provide clues to problem areas.
	• When you have surfaced the issue, help them solve their problem with a decision.
	• At times, their reservations will be about you. If so, acknowledge any past problems and state relevant data non-defensively, propose a plan and ask for help.
	• If you are not part of the problem, concentrate on helping the indecisive examine the facts. Use the facts to place alternative solutions in priority order. This makes it easier if they have to turn someone else down.
	• If real, emphasize the quality and service aspects of your proposal.
	• Give support after the decision seems to have been made.
	• If possible, keep the action steps in hand.
	• Watch for signs of abrupt anger or withdrawal from the conversation. If you see these try to remove them from the decision situation.

Summary points

- There are seven main types of difficult people that you will have to deal with: 1) hostile and aggressive people, 2) people who complain, 3) unresponsive, silent people, 4) over-agreeable people, 5) negative people, 6) know-it-alls and 7) indecisive people.

- You probably will find some types of difficult people more difficult to deal with than others. If you can recognize which, you can work on how to deal with that type.

- Each type of difficult person comes with specific responses that can diffuse the situation – so adequately diagnosing which category people belong to is crucial.

03
Dealing with difficult bosses

The brain is a wonderful organ; it starts working the moment you get up in the morning and doesn't stop until you get to the office.

ROBERT FROST

People get promoted and become the boss for all kinds of reasons. Some do so because they are really good at what they do, manage people and situations well, have a good grasp of the wider picture and can communicate ideas easily. That's the boss from heaven. Unfortunately, many bosses are from hell! But let's think about some scenarios that might have led to this situation.

- In technically oriented companies bosses might be promoted in light of their technical knowledge. But, when it comes to people, they may not necessarily have the people skills needed to manage a team.

- In family businesses, another family member might take over the position as a matter of course.

- In corporations bosses might get promoted as part of a pre-determined development path, rather than because they have reached the level of competency required.

- In some of the less attractive industries and public services, bosses who couldn't get a job anywhere else are common.

- In sales environments successful sales people might leave behind what they are good at, stop selling and make a mess of the detail needed to be a good boss.

- In companies where there are problems, an accountant emerges as the boss.
- In a fast-growing boom business scenario, perhaps the boss might not be as experienced as he/she could be.

Is there anywhere where a good boss can be found? Yes, of course there is. But it is worth making the point that bosses are not always promoted because they are good at being the boss. Being good at something, having good technical skills or having worked in an organization for a long time is often the passport to having 'Boss' written on the door. For some, the job makes the man or woman. Others become walking nightmares.

Inside every poor boss is a voice that tells the boss they are a poor boss. So, what do poor bosses do? They compensate. They overcome their insecurity by becoming caricatures of what they think a boss should be. If no one has ever trained them in people management, workforce skills or dealing with human resources, how are they to know? So they make it up. They become arrogant, belligerent, they shout, scream and manipulate. They are difficult to please, selfish and insecure. And very easy to deal with!

First things first. They are the boss and they can show you the door. So if you quite like the idea of hanging on to your salary at the end of the month, remember to be diplomatic. Let them feel they are in control – even if you are!

The angry boss

What do you do if you find yourself working for the angry type of boss? Easy. Let them get angry! What's it to you if they want to have a tantrum? It seldom lasts for more than a few minutes. Let them boil over, erupt and explode. As long as you don't join in, you're safe. Even if you are 100 per cent right, have company policy, the law, the European Court of Human Rights and all the angels in heaven on your side, don't join in.

> **Tip**
>
> The trick is to make yourself scarce until it blows over. Here's what you do. Say:
>
> *'I'm sorry you're so cross about this, but we need to deal with it rationally. I'm going to leave now and perhaps I can come back later when we've both had a chance to think it through.'*

Then leave. Whatever they say, leave. If they seem contrite, apologetic, even angrier, or want you to stay – leave. If necessary, say, 'No, *I want to leave it for now and perhaps I can come back in an hour or so and we'll look at it again.*'

Don't be tempted to have a row. It might be nice to fantasize about saying, 'You are so rude how do expect anyone to work with you? All you do is fly off the handle.' But then you have another problem to deal with – where are you working next week? Stay cool and deal with the issue on your terms.

> **Tip**
>
> The important word here is 'we'. It keeps you connected with events, shares the responsibility for what is happening and doesn't look like you are apportioning blame or being condemnatory. 'We' does nothing to inflame the situation.

Never let them see you sweat

Bully bosses like to see their staff sweat – so don't give them the pleasure. Whatever happens:

- Stay calm.

- Don't scream back.

- Don't get into an argument. Don't tell them what to do with their job. Telling them what they can do with their job may be very satisfying for 60 seconds but you'll regret it!

- And, never, never, never walk out on the spur of the moment.

Exercise

Bet you 20:1 this works…

This really does work. But I know you'll read this and groan. Trust me. It isn't magic, it isn't new and it isn't based on the latest psycho-fad. But, it is founded on the very good principles of stress and anger management.

Here it is: get away from the scene, argument, or whatever. Get on your own and count backwards from 20 to 1.

Take a deep breath, concentrate and count: 20, 19, 18, 17, 16, 15, 14, 13, 12, 11, 10, 9, 8, 7, 6, 5, 4, 3, 2, 1.

For some reason counting upwards doesn't work. Counting backwards does. It has a calming influence. Ever seen a stage hypnotist at work? They always use the backward counting technique to relax their victims.

Actually, there are some very good psychological reasons why it does work, but now is not the time and place! When you next feel like the deputy prime minister who gave an egg-chucker a straight left, try the 20 to 1 trick – odds on it will work for you.

When all else fails, what next?

OK, so you've done everything you can:

- You've delivered everything on time.

- When you couldn't deliver, you had a good reason and flagged up in advance that a deadline wasn't feasible.

- You've supported your boss in public, never been abusive and never made them look a fool, even if they are.

- You've worked with your boss, found out what gets them wound up and worked around it, over it and under it.

- You've never given them any ammunition to shoot you with.

What next?

You could try mediation.

- The human resource department may be able to help.

- You could appeal to a more senior member of staff to help you.

Tip

You could appeal to your boss with something like this:

'Look, I know we are all under a lot of pressure in this job and I can understand that means sometimes everyday niceties have to go by the board. However, I really don't think it is reasonable of you to expect me to put up with your behaviour and [describe a particular issue or incident so there is no ambiguity about what you are saying]. We are going to have to find a better basis of working together.'

In the end – what?

You only get one life and it is not (in a cliché worth a rerun) 'a rehearsal'. Leave, go, quit, get a life. If you are good at what you do, bail out and find another job. Do it on your terms, in your own time and at your own pace. Don't walk out, don't slam doors and don't threaten anything. Just leave. If you think you have a case for an industrial relations tribunal, visit your local Citizen's Advice Bureau and find out. Leave quietly. Don't tell people you're looking for another job: there is no such thing as a secret. Don't be unhappy, life is too short.

Exercise

Have you dealt with any of the difficult bosses we have talked about? How might you deal with them differently as a result of reading this chapter?

Summary points

- It is not uncommon to have difficult people placed in positions of authority; but just because they're the boss doesn't mean they're good at being the boss.

- Never enter a conflict with the boss: leave, diffuse the situation, appeal to other reasonable parties, but don't let them drag you into a conflict. They will win. They are the boss!

04
Dealing with difficult colleagues

> One of the saddest things is that the only thing you can do for
> eight hours a day, day after day, is work. You can't eat eight
> hours a day nor drink for eight hours a day nor make love
> eight hours a day.
>
> WILLIAM FAULKNER

Open-plan offices, team working, group targets, syndicated bonuses. Shift working with hand-over responsibilities, production line manufacturing based on mutual performance. The direction of modern business is to have people working closer together – both physically and mentally. And spiritually for that matter!

Tip

Working with people means just that. It also means working, sometimes, with difficult people.

Very few of us have the luxury of being able to retreat into the solitude of our own office, shut the door and be quiet for a few minutes. For most of us the workplace is crowded, busy, bustling and often noisy. The canteen is just the same and the locker room is probably worse. The quietest place is probably the loo!

Tip

Good workplace relationships are pivotal to company performance, and good managers and bosses understand that. The really good ones are not afraid to sort problems out – head on.

Competition crazy

Managers often mistake the roll of competition within a company. Perhaps one of the best examples of an oxymoron comes from the management lexicon: 'friendly competition', a complete contradiction in terms. There is no such thing and it does not encourage performance. It does encourage intrigue, conspiracy, back-stabbing, and focuses attention on scoring rather than winning.

Collaborating to win and competing to beat companies in the outside world who are after your customers is a better recipe.

You can choose your friends, you can choose the neighbourhood you want to live in. You can choose where to spend your money and you can choose your partner. You can choose your job. The two things you can't choose are the two groups most likely to give you trouble! You can't choose your family and you can't choose your colleagues.

Got your head around that? So get it into perspective. Once you've come to terms with that, the rest is easy. Expect, from time to time, difficulties to arise. It would be a miracle if they didn't! If they don't, sit back and think how lucky you are.

Exercise

Sales people! Can there be a more difficult group of people in the whole universe? You're dealing with high self-esteem, low self-esteem, arrogance, belligerence, pride, egoism, conceit, persistence, courage, confidence, perseverance, stamina and tenacity. A cocktail of just about every human emotion you can think of. Then someone comes along and says, 'Motivate the sales team.'

How? There is a group of men and women who are all different, in terms of their emotional and psychological states, highs and lows, peaks and troughs, complex home lives, personal disasters, challenges and happiness. It takes a brave person to think there is a magic trick that will motivate 'the sales team'!

If you were tasked with this challenge, how would you consider harnessing such high levels of competitiveness and improving outcomes?

Jot down some ideas and then turn to the end of the book to see what happened when I was given this job to do.

Are there difficult people that you work with where a different approach would help?

Rivals, antagonists and getting personal

Personal attacks don't work. They leave behind a stain on a relationship which can take forever to remove. People harbour grudges, bitterness and resentment, and these get in the way of the work that needs to be done.

> **Tip**
>
> Never let it get personal. Separate the issue from the person. Decouple the individual from the difficulty. Divide the personality from the problem.

Better not say, 'Because of the way you've handled this, we are now in a real *%##^$ mess', even if it's true! All that will happen is that the individual will spend the next three hours defending themself, their department, mother, family and the good Lord in heaven. It won't solve the problem. The problem is fixing the issue. So concentrate on the issue.

Let's think about this. This 'don't let it get personal' approach is right out of the pages of so-called conflict resolution.

Try, *'We need to get this sorted, so let's look at [the issue] and agree the next step.'*

> **Tip**
>
> If someone tries to take the conversation back to whose fault it was, or goes down the road of name recrimination, bring them back on track fast. *'How we got into this situation is less important to us right now than seeing our way through it. Let's decide where we go from here.'*

It's always the quiet ones

Ever been in a meeting where some people sat still and said nothing? Ever wondered why? Let's think about some possible reasons for this:

- Are they shy?
- Perhaps they are embarrassed?

- Do they think they are too good for this place and you aren't worth bothering with?

- Maybe they need a little confidence to get going. Perhaps they feel superior and don't want to intervene. It could be they need 'permission' to participate. It might be they are conspiring against you! (Included as an outside possibility, just to entertain the paranoid few!)

You know where you are with colleagues who blow their stack, are critical, or are keen to have a row. But where are you with the quiet ones?

Whatever the problem, here's a way to coax them, get them going or smoke them out.

Exercise

Try this approach next time you are in a meeting with an overly quiet colleague.

Ask for their opinion on a less important part of the overall topic. Simple questions that they will find easy to answer and look really incompetent if they don't. Don't stop with one question. As the meeting progresses, ask them two or three questions, of a similar type.

What happened? Was it one of these typical outcomes and what does this tell you about your colleague?

- The shy ones will be coaxed into making a contribution.

- The 'I am too good for this meeting' types will disdainfully answer the easy questions and will not be able to resist making a more high-powered intervention.

- The conspirators will answer the question and stay quiet. Look out for them!

Summary points

- You can't choose your colleagues and yet you probably spend the most time out of your day with them – accept this fact and move on.

- Never let a sense of competition creep in between you and your colleagues. You should be collaborating instead to beat the competition from outside the organization.

- Never let it get personal; separate the issue from the person.

05
Dealing with difficult staff

I should have worked just long enough to discover I didn't like it.

PAUL THEROUX

So, you've made it: you're somebody's boss. Well done.

Ain't being the boss fun? Well, it should be! In truth it's not easy. Even though you are the boss, there will still be pressures on you. Figure 5.1 shows how this works.

> ### Tip
>
> At the heart of every employee relationship problem I have ever looked at lurked a 13-letter word: communication. Thirteen, got it? Unlucky for some – how about you?

In the annoying jargon of the management guru, all bosses have to manage down and manage up. Wouldn't your life be much easier if you didn't have to worry about the people? A business without staff – pure joy! (We'll get on to the customers later.)

Somehow you have to find a formula that maximizes the productivity of the organization and gets the best out of the staff you have – without being a slave driver or turning into a problem boss.

Figure 5.1   Pressure at each level

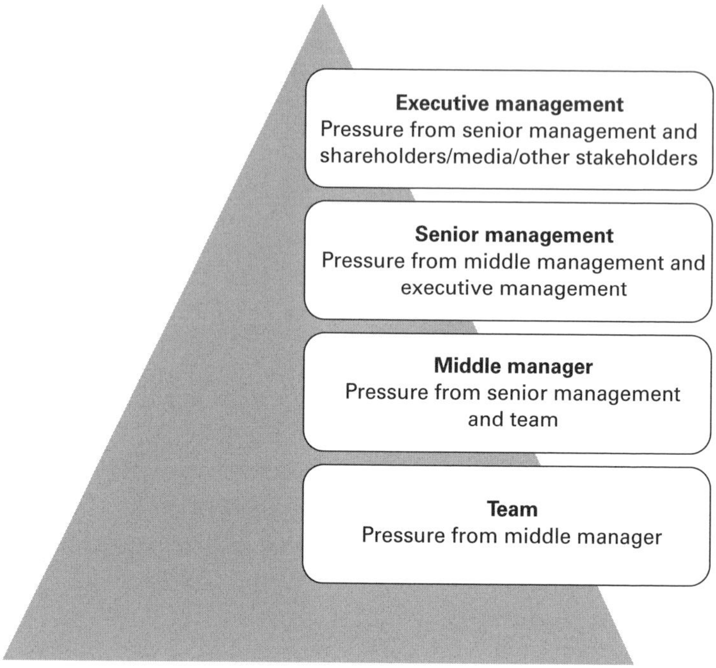

Executive management
Pressure from senior management and
shareholders/media/other stakeholders

Senior management
Pressure from middle management and
executive management

Middle manager
Pressure from senior management
and team

Team
Pressure from middle manager

Tip

Communication and understanding are the ways to avoid dealing
with difficult staff. Tell people what you want and expect from
them, spell out how you want something done, and be clear
about targets and objectives.

Exercise

Consider the following comments made by staff:

- 'You don't understand the pressures on the department.'

- 'No one told me what the deadline for this order was. I thought next week would be OK.'

- 'I didn't know you wanted it done differently, I always do it like that.'

Jot down some ideas as to how these outcomes could have been avoided.

Tip

No one ever ran a successful business sitting behind a desk.

Tip

If you don't take the time to tell people what you want, how do you expect they will ever be able to give you what you want?

The really world-class businessmen and -women in the UK are few and far between. The top-drawer ones all have something in common. They are fanatical about getting out and about in their businesses. Here are some examples to consider:

- Lord Sieff built the world's best retailers, Marks & Spencer (yes, I know they may be approaching their sell-by date and they need a good shake-up to reflect the 21st century), by making sure he spent two days a week in the stores or at suppliers.

- Today Britain's best-known entrepreneur, Sir Richard Branson, is likely to turn up on one of his transatlantic planes, serving the drinks, or to sit next to you on one of his trains. He was also known to serve customers in his record stores.

- The guys who run the Carphone Warehouse show up at the shops. Rocco Forte, rebuilding his leisure empire, books into his hotels (under a pseudonym) several nights a week.

Tip

If you always do what you always do, you'll always get what you've got.

All the top business people do it. They realize they have to, to understand the business, to find out what customers really want and how the staff go about their jobs.

It's not just in the world of business either. In an effort to find out what it is like to be a patient in the NHS, Leicester NHS Trust puts trainee doctors in touch with patients with chronic conditions. They spend time with them and try to understand what it's like to be ill and frightened. They chaperone patients through accident and emergency departments and discover how awful it is to have to wait for hours to be attended to. They even stay in the homes of patients with long-term conditions, to understand the pressures there are on carers.

The BBC ran a fascinating series of programmes called *Back to the Floor*. Leading business types spent a week working on the 'shop floor' of their business.

They all ended up with a much deeper understanding of their business, and each of them was able to introduce changes to make the lives of his or her employees easier.

By finding out what the business was really like, they were able to communicate with their staff on the basis of a good understanding of what could be achieved. They all decided that what they were getting was not what they wanted, and changed the way they did things.

> **Tip**
>
> By understanding your business, you'll have fewer 'difficult' staff and customers to deal with.

Independent or stubborn?

Employees who solve problems, use their initiative and develop local answers to local problems are every good boss's dream. Encouraging operational independence is a great idea. But (sorry, there's always a 'but', isn't there?) when independence spills over into wilfulness and independence takes an employee off down a track of their own, it's time for the boss to act.

> **Exercise**
>
> Think about a time when you have felt a member of staff has been acting too independently. Ask yourself these questions:
>
> - Is it because I can't get my own way?
> - Am I jealous that they found a better way and I feel undermined?
> - Do I have a glorious dream that everyone has to be a team player and I've got no time for individuals?
> - Is it because the member of staff is damaging the business by doing their own thing?
>
> If you answered yes to any of the first three, you might want to consider who is the difficult person.

What is the real damage: your ego or the business process? You may have to accept that some staff, like Paul Anka's song, do it *My Way*. Is it screwing up the process, costing more than it should, affecting the productivity of the company, annoying other staff? Is it dangerous, putting people at risk? Or, is it a good idea you hadn't thought of?

Tip

Think before you act. If you do, act with justification and right on your side. Remember, the rule book and the procedures manual may not be your best ally, especially if the wayward member of staff has genuinely found a better way.

If and when you do decide to sort out the problem, try to do it without destroying the motivation of your victim. *'I know you are used to doing it your way, but the company has good reasons for wanting you to do it another way. Let me take you through what they are.'*

At the end of the encounter, add this bit: *'We are really keen to learn from the experience of the people actually doing the job. If you can come up with a better/safer/faster/more reliable way, let me know and we'll see how it fits into the whole picture and try to implement it. We like good ideas.'*

That way your staff member may go home reassured in the knowledge they are not dealing with a difficult boss!

When the big hand gets to 12

Ever thought why staff become clock-watchers?

- It could be they have problems at home.
- Maybe they look after a sick partner or an elderly relative.
- They may have to pick up their children from the crèche or childminder.

- Perhaps they have to catch a train or bus.

- Are they rushing off to evening classes or a secret assignation?

Who knows? You should! Shouldn't you? Leaving aside the assignation, shouldn't you know if your staff are under external pressure? Can you help? Change hours? Be a more family-friendly employer?

Perhaps there's another reason. Are they doing the job, or doing a good job of looking like they are doing the job? Could it be the job is mind-blowingly, eye-wateringly, brain-crunchingly dull, boring and depressing?

How do you judge them? Do they have potential? Do you want to give them a lift and motivate them? Of course you do. The modern workplace has refined and deskilled tasks to the point where work can be a drudge. Frequent breaks, swapping tasks and changing surroundings can all help to alleviate dreary jobs. Are you doing what you can?

Tip

How about giving this a try: *'I'd like to give you a change from the routine. Would you have a go at this for me…?'*

If it's not the work or the environment, the expectation is that it's personal.

To remind of you what I said earlier, 'No one ever ran a successful business sitting behind a desk.' If staff are undermotivated, clock-watching and performing poorly, how much of it can be attributed to the work, the working environment or the working methods?

Time to go back to the floor. Do the job yourself, find out what it's like. I'll bet real money that, in less than three days, you'll find a solution – or your money back!

Good bosses don't pry – but they should try

Loss of motivation, poor performance, lack of interest: which is it? There's only one way to find out. If you are satisfied it isn't a workplace issue, ask!

> *'I can see you're not getting much out of being at work these days. Is there something going on we can help you with?'*

Expect the reply, 'No, nothing. I'm all right.'

> *'That's fine. I just wanted you to know that if there were something, my door is open and we can chat if you want to.'*

You'll maybe get an answer, or a clue. Perhaps nothing. You may get an approach at a later time. Be patient. The important thing is, you've sent a signal, one that says, we'd be happier if you were happier. More than that you can't do.

Waving or drowning

Have you ever had high hopes for a member of staff, then discovered they just can't hack it? Ask yourself why.

- Were they recruited badly, with not enough research into career experience and background?
- Has the job shifted into more testing territory?
- Have they got a personal problem that is on their mind?
- Are they in debt?
- Are their kids playing up?

Whatever it is, you're the boss. Dealing with difficult people and tricky situations is down to you. Get on with it!

If it's a personal problem, here are some options:

- Do you need to organize some training?
- Is the job too easy, so the individual is under-performing because they are not challenged?
- Did the person give a false impression at interview, or were they perhaps untruthful about their experience?
- Did referees lie?
- Can you reorganize the process?
- Can you shift some of the workload onto someone else for a while, to let the employee get up to speed?
- Do you need to review your recruitment processes?

Next, talk to the person. Do it in the context of the original job interview.

- Get out the paperwork.
- Go over their experience and qualifications.
- Take a view as to whether they should be coping better.

Agree training, or a respite period and a timetable for improvement. Review it regularly. If there is no real improvement, shift the individual to a less demanding role, or if you have to, let them go.

Tip

If you think you are at the point where you need to let a staff member go, talk to your line manager and/or HR before you take action.

It's difficult, but kinder in the long run.

When you've finished hitting people with the stick, try hitting them with the carrots.

Workplace rewards, bonuses, productivity payments, cash incentives are all part of the modern workplace. For some staff they are just right. When you say 'Jump', if the bonus is good enough, they'll ask, 'How high?'

Research shows that people work for more than money, and quite a high percentage of staff are not motivated by money.

This is particularly true of many public service workers who have a concept of principled motivation. They are driven by a service ethos and set great store by training opportunities and personal, professional development.

They are into something called pride-in-a-job-well-done. They're worried about the embarrassment or shame if they don't hit a target. Job satisfaction plays a big part in what motivates staff.

Tip

If you throw a big commission or bonus package into the office don't expect everyone to grab it. Different people are motivated differently.

Exercise

Try this approach with your staff. You can use the grid below as a template/checklist.

Have you	Y/N
Arranged a private meeting area, where both of you can be seated and have a one-to-one conversation?	
Explained the overall goal?	
Made sure the individual understands the overall goal and their level of contribution?	
Explained expected performance levels and individual goals?	
Ensured the individual understands the expected performance levels and individual goals?	

Have you	Y/N
Made sure you encourage staff to stretch themselves? (But remember that being over-ambitious and setting unrealistic goals is no good for the company and very demotivating for the member of staff who fails to reach them.)	
Agreed to arrange regular sessions to monitor performance? (Be prepared to modify goals by mutual arrangement, but otherwise stick to the rule.)	

After taking this approach with some members of staff, review how effective the process has been.

Personal rewards are not always the answer. Some people are motivated by what they can achieve for others.

Don't forget the possibility of linking performance to donations to a charity or other good cause.

Use the 'stick' to hold a person to their agreed objectives. Use the carrot to say well done.

Finding out how good a boss you've been

How's your back? Been stabbed lately? Unsuspecting bosses will have staff who are nice to their face and horrible the moment they are out of the office.

The first question is do you deserve it? Be honest with yourself: what sort of a boss are you? If you are satisfied you are not the boss from hell (if you are not sure, read the section at the beginning of the book. Recognize anyone?), then you'll have to act.

Tip

You could consider asking your staff for formal feedback. Many organizations support this approach. Your line manager or HR department should be able to tell you if a process is in place for this kind of feedback.

It is not just a personal thing. Staff who bitch about their bosses with no justification play hell with the reputation of the company and the morale of staff, especially junior members.

Feel that stabbing pain between the shoulderblades? Try this:

'What you think about me personally is up to you. However, we're not here for fun. There is a business to run and I do the best I can to run it. If you have a legitimate criticism of me, come and talk to me privately and directly. My door is open to you. Otherwise, keep your offensive remarks to yourself.'

Tough? Yes, but that's why you're the boss. The other staff will soon realize what's happened and will probably be relieved they don't have to listen to the rubbish. More, you'll go up in their estimation for dealing with it.

Seriously difficult members of staff

This is not the book to teach you about employment law and industrial tribunals, but you do need to know your stuff, or know someone who does. That's why they pay you so much money!

Employment law is based on evidence. In recent years there have been huge shifts in the balance between the employee and the employer. This is a good thing. No one wants to work in, or run, a sweatshop. The law is complex and a minefield for the unwary.

For operational purposes, the key phrases are: write everything down, keep contemporaneous notes, and hang on to evidence.

The golden rule is to deal with difficult issues as swiftly as you can.

Tip

A rule that comes from the time-management gurus is good for those trying to deal with a difficult member of staff; make the job you least want to do your first job.

Don't wait, don't let situations fester. Deal with it, no matter how difficult it is and no matter how reluctant you are and no matter how horrible it's going to be. Apply the JGDI rule: just go do it!

Employment law is stuff for experts. If you are a new boss, or a boss not sure of your ground, find out about company policy, talk to the human resources people and don't be shy about being ignorant. This is not the time or place for an enthusiastic amateur. If you are a self-employed boss, the Citizens Advice Bureau, the local job centre and books like Croner's *CCH Employment Law Manual* will point you in the right direction. If in doubt, ask a lawyer.

Exercise

Spend some time on the Acas website. Understand the basics of employment law and review what you have learned alongside your company policy. Make a note of anything that you do not understand or would like to discuss in more detail and ask your line manager or HR department if they can help you.

Summary points

- Now that you're the boss, minimize the risk of difficult people being allowed to become problematic by communicating. Tell your people clearly what is expected of them and how they are expected to get to those goals.

- Understanding the realities your staff face will help you adequately deal with them, and give them the right environment so that problems don't arise in the first place. Understand your staff, your business and your clients.

- Be flexible to different ways of doing things. Your staff may know how to do things better.

- Often difficult people have extenuating circumstances that you, the boss, can attend to – try to do everything you can to help your staff and you will have less difficult people to work with.

- You may be able to improve a difficult employee's performance by correctly incentivizing them, but not everyone responds to the same type of incentives. Find out what's important to them.

- If the situation with a difficult employee starts having serious ramifications, always call the experts and check you are in line with employment law.

06
Massaging the egoist

One may understand the cosmos, but never the ego; the self is more distant than any star.

G K CHESTERTON

Successful people, to get where they are today, will have needed a bit of luck, a lot of courage, some knowledge and generally a great deal of effort.

They will be confident and they will be self-assured. They will be proud of their achievements and they will be positive. There is also the possibility that they could be egomaniacs!

Egoists, show-offs, the self-centred, the know-alls; or the insecure, the easily flattered and the attention seekers. It's not difficult at all. They're all easy to deal with.

If the difficulty is an egomaniac boss

It's easy; give the boss the credit! All right, not all the time. But you don't have to take the credit every time, do you? If you want to get your own way with an egoist, flattery is the easy way to do it. Got a great idea that you want to get past your egomaniac boss? Try this:

'I've read the memo you sent out about reorganizing the western division. You know, I think you're right. Taking what you said as the foundation, here's what I thought we might do...'

> **Tip**
>
> You'll never change the boss but you can change how people
> think about you. If you are good at what you do and shine, pretty
> soon everyone will know where the good ideas are coming from,
> so don't worry about one-upmanship.

Does this sound like giving in, giving up or rolling over? Only if
you're no good at your job. Egomaniac bosses can be seen (and
enjoyed) by all the employees, not just you.

If the difficulty is an egoist working for you

If you are trying to get a group of people to work together, behave
as a team and develop a close-knit motivation, the last thing you
want is an egomaniac grabbing the headlines for themselves. Give
this a try:

> 'Eleanor, I know you are working very hard and doing your
> best for us, but I am anxious to get everyone up to a high
> performance standard. I want you to make sure everyone gets
> their share of the credit. That way we all do better. Don't you
> agree?'

Getting Eleanor the egoist onside is easy. Just appeal to her ego: ask
for a little help to spread the praise.

The egomaniac colleague

Mr Perfect, Miss Right: mistake! But that's their problem. The
solution is to listen to them boast and puff themselves up and then

stick to the facts. Don't prick their bubble, just let them down slowly. Sticking to the facts and figures will do that for you. '*Well done. Just how many/how much did you actually do to achieve whatever…?*' No matter what they say, you've sent a signal. Loud and clear you are saying that you're not interested in the bull, you're interested in the meat. They will soon stop boasting if they know you are the type of person who will want the facts to back up their bragging.

Knocking the know-all

This is tricky; remember, you have to work with these people!

Get the facts and go for it: '*I'm not sure you're being quite accurate there, Edward. I've had a look at the records and actually…*' Edward and his ego nicely fall flat on their backs. Don't try to out-ego the egoist and don't try to beat them up. Just go for the facts and let these do the work.

Exercise

Have you ever encountered people who were difficult because their ego got in the way of your working relationship? Reflect on how some of the techniques suggested could help improve the situation.

Egoists are easy to put down. Just deny them the oxygen of attention and they will wither away. Is that what you want? If the idea is to get the best out of people, the odd compliment, the occasional pat on the back and some recognition once in a while should keep them on the team and make the situation manageable.

Summary points

- If you have to deal with an egotistical boss, flatter them when possible but keep them at a distance.

- If you have to deal with an egotistical employee, make sure they know you care about team performance as well.

- If you have to deal with an egotistical colleague or know-it-all, always ask them to back up their claims. Better yet, have the facts ready to assist your arguments.

07
Handling aggressive people

Nobody ever forgets where they buried the hatchet.

KIN HUBBARD

This not about physical aggression, this is about the kind of aggression that masks performance or hides bad behaviour. Sometimes tactless people can appear aggressive, as can the sarcastic. They have the sort of 'gets under your skin' behaviour that begs you to plant a left hook.

This is not the time or place for a dissertation on psychiatry. The seeds of this sort of behaviour can be deeply planted, so let's not spend time trying to dig them up. What is needed is to achieve what you want to achieve and move forward.

Be clear about your objectives, get the facts on your side and look for outcomes to measure.

Aggression takes on several guises. Hypocrisy, condescension, double-dealing, sabotage, bullying, set-ups, unwarranted criticism, delegation to the point where you are snowed under: they are all there somewhere.

One answer is to perform out of your socks, stick to the facts and hope pretty soon the boss will recognize what's going on.

Let's think about this. Aggressive folks are often very critical. Be sure not to reject criticism out of hand. They might be right.

Criticism from customers must be listened to. Criticism from junior colleagues is worth attending to: think how much courage it has taken for them to face you.

Tip

If you can get to the mind-set where criticism is as valuable to you as a compliment, you've cracked it.

If an aggressive manager is trying to dump on your ideas

They'll try to drown you in details, suffocate you with demands for statistics. They'll pulverize you with planning, more planning and re-planning, terrify you with tales of how it will never work and the terrible consequences. Try this. See if it is possible to downsize your idea, be less ambitious:

'Could we pilot the idea for a couple of months, in one territory and see how it goes? We can evaluate it and see if it is worth rolling out across the rest of the area later.'

If you're landed with a project that will never fly

One sneaky tactic of the aggressive manager is to dump you with a project that will never work and let you take the blame for failure. Try to widen the number of people who could end up looking stupid.

'Goodness knows why we've ended up with this. It's obvious that it's a no-hoper. Everyone is going to look stupid, finance, *corporate, production and middle management. Shouldn't we get together and decide what we're going to do?'*

Does anyone else feel the same as you? Have a quiet word with trusted colleagues; *'Maybe it's just me but, I think Andrew is very aggressive and I find it very daunting to deal with. How do you feel?'*

Find some allies and deal with the problem together.

If you're being stabbed in the back

This is the favourite ploy of the aggressive manager or colleague. Thought you had their support? Thought they were behind you? Well, they were, at least until there was a problem. Now, they've disappeared.

What next? Clever, calculated and cunning confrontation is called for! *'I thought we had agreed our approach here and that there were five things we needed to do. I remember we talked about it.'* The person is bound to say, *'No, I never signed up to any of that.'* It's time for some salvage. *'Look, there is no point in arguing about it. Let's sort out what we can agree on and move on. How about this and this and this?'*

Exercise

Don't be caught out twice. This kind of behaviour is very hard to stop in its tracks. Be prepared to work around it. First rule: make notes. When you have a planning meeting, formal or informal, make notes. If there are no formal minutes, make your own notes. Date them and keep them. Next time there is a problem: bingo! Produce your notes. It will make the stabbers and the hypocrites think twice before they mess with you again.

Summary points

- Never escalate conflict with someone who is aggressive. Stick to the facts and your guns and try to defuse the situation.

- If your work is being unfairly criticized by a manager, try to gain some time and let the results speak for themselves.

- Always stick to the facts and document everything so you can come back with real proof for your arguments backing up your work.

08
Dealing with laziness

He has his law degree and a furnished office. It's just a question, now, of getting him out of bed.

PETER ARNO

Why do people get lazy? We know work can be routine, monotonous, tedious and uninteresting. Employees who start out being diligent and productive can be hypnotized into inactivity, simply by the nature of what they are doing.

Re-engineer the task, change the approach and let the staff, if you can, have a big say in the working environment and the way they approach it.

Don't be afraid to challenge laziness:

'Justin, you seem to be having a lot of problems getting your projects finished on time. You know we have to depend on you delivering. What can we do to make you more reliable?'

The subtlety here is to turn the criticism into a question. 'Why are you always late delivering?' is designed to invite a whole load of excuses, waffle, rebuttal and aggravation. 'You seem to be having trouble, what can we do about it?' focuses the energy in a different direction and invites a more positive response.

Whose fault is it anyway? Are the staff lazy or poorly managed? You won't get five-star performance if people don't know what they are supposed to be doing.

> **Tip**
>
> Have you given clear instructions? Is what you are asking realistic? Is there any confusion about what is expected?

Clock-watchers, rule-bookers and not invented here

This is about motivation: making people tick faster than the clock. Have a good look at the way people are working. If you can, spend some time doing the job yourself. That way you'll have a good idea what's wrong and what you can do about it.

What can you change? The environment? The process? The times? The schedules? The materials? The tools? The equipment? The breaks? The clothing? The music? Wherever you can, involve the lazy lot. Introduce ideas to engage staff:

- team-based solution meetings;
- team bonuses;
- group quality initiatives;
- rotating jobs.

Do the staff see the whole process or do they just see 'their bit' of the production? Widen their interest by opening up the whole process. Do the staff ever talk to the customer or end-user of the process or service?

When the importance of their role in the process is emphasized, staff often find a new motivation.

Exercise

Which of these would most likely work best for your team and why?

- Team-based solution meetings.
- Team bonuses.
- Group quality initiatives.
- Rotating jobs.

Could you make an action plan to introduce any of these ideas? What might be the pros and cons?

If you are held back by an idle colleague

Are they just disorganized? Can you get them better organized? Help them to time manage. Lead by example. Getting into the detail may help. Prepare a detailed list or schedule, review points and outcome measurements. Make sure they understand the delivery points, what they have to do and what part they are playing. Use milestones to move your millstone. If all else fails:

'Janet, I really want to get this project delivered on time. We are running late and I'm still waiting for your work/ production/input. Shouldn't we sit down together and make a timetable that we can both live with and be sure of delivering?'

Got a colleague who is always late? Start without them. When they arrive, make them catch up. They'll soon learn.

A boss who loiters

Delays, dithering, procrastination, stalling, dawdling? Putting decisions back into the in-tray? Why do they do it? Infuriating, isn't it? There are a lot of reasons why bosses don't cut the mustard. They may be out of their depth. They may be short on some information. They may not have the same priorities as you. The answer is to help them out. Do they need some background work, some research, someone to be a gofer?

There's the answer. Do it for them. Help to make making the decisions easier. This may mean more work, but to get a project moving and finished it might be worth looking at your extra work as an investment.

Be subtle and get it right and you become indispensable. You also run the risk of being put-upon, dumped on and exploited. Your call…

Tip

Take care not to overstep your authority. Don't make the decision, just line up the facts and figures so that the decision can be made with the minimum of effort and risk.

How you eat an elephant

American management guru Tom Peters, in his book *In Search of Excellence*, gives us the answer: elephant burgers, elephant steak, elephant stew, elephant risotto, elephant kebab. Get the idea?

If people are swamped by the size of the task they will often withdraw, dawdle, procrastinate and get to look (and be) lazy. The answer is to break the job up into bite-size segments, and agree and set priorities and deadlines. Stay in touch and on top of the project, and be ruthless in insisting deadlines are met.

Look out for employees who delight in appearing swamped, overworked and with an in-tray that would take 10 strong men to lift. They are probably not lazy. When they are waving for attention it probably means they are drowning. Help them, teach them to prioritize. Rip this out and stick it on the notice board in the office:

> Success by a yard is hard. Success by an inch is a synch.

The exceptionally lazy

They have 'lazy' to an art form. They will whine, plead, grizzle, moan, conspire and devote the energy it takes to run 10 power stations to avoid doing the job.

It takes a lot of energy to be lazy, keep a job and not get caught. It needs planning, forethought, charm, effort, energy, determination, intelligence, originality, guile and judgement: all the things needed for success and to be a five-star employee.

Perhaps there are no lazy staff, just bad bosses?

Summary points

- Counteract lazy employees by trying to find out how to motivate and engage them in their work – can you change their work environment or how they feel about their jobs?

- Help your lazy team member learn by adjusting how you treat them.

- Where possible, don't wait for lazy bosses to do the job – do it yourself.

- Break down huge tasks for lazy people to deal with so they feel they progress through a to-do list more quickly.

09
Beating the bullies at their own game

There is nothing ignoble in loving one's enemies – but there is much that is dangerous.

BERNARD LEVIN

Let's face it, Attila the Hun got things done. Genghis Khan went places. Working for either of them wasn't exactly a bowl of cherries.

Bosses do think (or some bosses do) that the best boss is the boss who shouts the loudest, slams the doors and frightens everyone out of their wits.

Tip

Tyrants want a fight and bullies love a victim. There's the clue in what to do with a bully for a boss. Don't fight and don't be a victim.

Bullies become bullies because they find they can get away with it, and bullies are bullies because they have no other management technique. Lack of skills, insight, insecurity and incompetence turns bad bosses into bully bosses.

If bullies need a victim, why are you a victim? You need a job? Sure, we all do. You need to pay the bills? Yup, of course. But you only have one life, so don't spend it in fear.

If you've tried everything and life is still hell, what next?

Shouldn't you be taking your time and quietly, subtly and decisively looking for another job?

The decibel dictator

How do you deal with the screamer, the abuser, the table-thumper? Stay calm, unemotional and objective.

'I know you are concerned about this, and of course it needs to be sorted out, but shouting at me/abusing me is not going to solve the problem. It is very unsettling and upsetting and won't make me work any better.'

Very straight to the point.

What next? The boss will need a way to climb down, so expect a follow-up tirade of less intensity and of the self-justification type: 'Just as long as you understand the importance of all this... blah, blah.'

Answer, *'I do, so let's concentrate on the issues. What is the first step?'*

Tip

Made a foul-up? Admit it, don't fudge it, apologize and offer to work to put things right. That's common sense. Are you being wrongly accused? Then try, *'You need to know the following three facts. The work is not completed because 1..., 2..., 3...'*

When all else fails

The boss has lost it. The screaming can be heard in mainland Europe and the rest of the staff have run for cover. What do you do? Cower, hide, cringe, tremble, quake, shrink? Go to the boss's boss? That's risky.

Bully bosses often mimic behaviour. They get it from their boss.

If your boss's boss is a bully, the chances are your boss will be a bully. It'll be accepted behaviour and part of the organization culture, so appealing to a higher authority is likely to prove an unfruitful tactic.

What to do? In truth, find another job. You don't need it. You're too good.

Stay as calm as a cucumber and try this. '*Mr Bulstrode, sit down/ still and think.*' I'll bet Bulstrode will shut up (or your money back). Continue, '*You are upset and I can see why, but you have no right to talk to me like that [use that language/say those things]. If you want to continue this, talk to me in a civil way and we can sort out the problem.*' Then say nothing, look as neutral and unflustered as you can and wait. Bulstrode will have to back off.

Don't stay and be the victim. Get out of the firing line, and do it without blame, accusation or reproach. Say, 'Brian, I'll see you later', and clear off. Get out of there. Bullies need victims and audiences.

Tip

Try to major on the issues and not the behaviour.

The firework colleague

What lights their touch-paper? One minute they're cuddly and workable-with, the next they are a Chinese firecracker. Can you detect what sets them off? If you can, keep off the topic, or issue. When the fireworks start, obey the four golden rules:

- Don't accuse – it adds fuel to the fire.

- Don't say things like 'Calm down' – it'll exacerbate things.

- Don't join in – you'll prolong it.

- Don't stay in the firing line – it's not safe.

Tip

When the dust settles, don't get into recriminations. Move on: *'I know this is important. Let's sort it out together because together we're more likely to succeed.'*

Feeling intimidated? If you are feeling intimidated, the chances are you are being intimidated. This kind of fear is insidious. Ask yourself why you're feeling intimidated. Do you feel insecure, inadequate, not up to the job, got something to hide? How we react to people starts within ourselves. If we want to be a victim, then we will be. If we let people push us around, they will.

If you are on top of the job, doing the best you can, you have no reason to feel intimidated. Don't expect logic to play any part in this human relations equation. Bullies are not logical, they are opportunistic and unpredictable. Your defences are your talent, skill, patience and coolness under fire. Avoid the emotions and stick to the facts. Stay away from the passion and follow a plan.

Exercise

Bullying in the workplace is a serious issue. Visit the Acas website and spend some time understanding what constitutes bullying in the workplace and their advice on how to deal with it.

Summary points

- If your boss is a bully, don't fight and don't be a victim.
- If your boss screams and gets angry, defuse the situation and wait to try and reason with them. Reason only when they are in a fit state to reason.
- If all else fails and you're being intimidated, recognize that sometimes nothing can be done.

10
Moaners, groaners and critics

Never pay attention to what critics say. A statue has never been set up in honour of a critic.

JEAN SIBELIUS

In a perfect world we'd all be perfect and there would be nothing to moan about, nothing to grumble about and nothing to criticize. As it stands, it is not (yet) a perfect world, things will go wrong, there will be foul-ups, mistakes and blunders. So expect moaners, groaners and critics.

Constructive criticism, delivered with sincerity and in the spirit of doing things better, is no bad thing. Some bosses take it too far, mainly because they're not very good at being a boss. But then who is?

If you are stuck with a critical boss, your best defence is to stick with the facts. If they grumble, produce the notes, the memos, the work, the invoice, the plan, the meeting minutes. Like the man in the US detective television programme used to say, 'Stick to the facts, ma'am.'

Overly serious bosses can fall into the trap of taking great performance for granted and majoring on the times when things go wrong. Don't be the wrong sort of boss. Try not to be overly serious!

If the facts don't come out on your side, admit the mistake, offer to put it right and agree a course of action to make sure it doesn't happen again. If you've got a grizzly boss and you know there is a foul-up, the best advice is to get in first. Be proactive and confess:

> 'I'm not really sure how this happened, and we'll have to look into it to find out, but the William's account is late on delivery. May I suggest we take the following action to put it right, look into how it happened and make some arrangements to ensure that this type of thing is not overlooked again. I'm really sorry.'

This may not save you from a roasting but it might save you from getting fired.

Cold water torture

It's not just bosses who can be a pain. Colleagues can consistently try to trash your great ideas. Try getting them onside by having a private word. You'll get to know the kind of thing that makes them turn negative; think about it and add it to the equation. Work around the negativity. Negative people are often insecure people who are not inventive and not creative. In the face of inventive people and creative types they feel their own limitations and try to make up for the difference by stamping all over your ideas.

Tip

Try sharing your ideas with with negative people. Get them onside by offering co-ownership of a project you want to get through.

Try building alliances, coalitions and connections

Peddle your ideas around colleagues, ask for opinions, champions and white knights. Get friends onside and positive feedback before involving the grumpy one. Be sure to reveal your idea when your supporters are present. The moaners and the groaners often disappear when they find they have no allies.

Tip

Not keen on the idea of sharing the idea? Is it better to give away some of the praise to get the idea off the ground? Sharing the credit might make the idea fly.

Exercise

Keep a tally chart, over a day, or even a week. Record negative reactions and try the responses provided below.

Negative reaction	Tally	Response
Nothing like that can be done		Oh dear, I'm sorry to hear that. Tell me why you say that. How can you be sure this particular plan won't work?
We tried that before and got into a real mess		Yes, I know. I looked at the Mark II project and have been careful to avoid the pitfalls that trapped that team. Let me explain how this is different...

Negative reaction	Tally	Response
Why do we need to bother with all that?		This approach saves money/time/effort/ makes a better widget/is faster/more thorough. [Sell the benefits.] Let me explain how...
We don't do things like that here		I know we don't, but I think we should start. Let me explain why...

How did you get on?

When critics turn the gun on themselves

Criticism is contagious. Add an organization's capacity to create gossip and you're soon dealing with an epidemic. If the criticism is well founded, don't be precious, take it on board and deal with it, and let everyone know you've done so. Otherwise, try to get the arch-critic on board. *'Damon, I know you'll have some strong opinions on this, so before I go public I want to have your views.'* Approaching it this way gives you two chances. First, you'll know what the arguments will be and you can prepare. Second, you might just end up with an ally.

Staff with little confidence will often be self-critical. They seem to think it's easier if they criticize themselves before someone else does. If you're the boss and have staff members like that, you must act.

Staff are any organization's most important asset. It is vital they are motivated, confident and encouraged. Take them to one side and say:

'It is a great shame to hear you talking like that. You have excellent skills/experience/energy/enthusiasm/loyalty... and I hate to hear you waste it. You're doing a good job. See, I've told you. Now tell yourself.'

Staff may put themselves down in the hope that someone will come along and tell them how great they are at their job. Don't get suckered into that one. Stick with, *'I think we both know what sort of job you're doing. If I didn't think you were good enough, you wouldn't be in the department/on the team, so let's stick to the facts.'*

Summary points

- If someone criticizes your work, stick with the facts. If the facts aren't on your side and you are in the wrong, be upfront about it, explain what went wrong and how you can fix it, how you'll do it differently next time and apologize.

- If your ideas are being met with resistance, try involving the difficult people in the discussion and crucially seek other allies that will be on your side and will strengthen your arguments.

- If you know someone will be critical, nip it in the bud. Deal with the criticism head on and before you involve other people in the discussion.

11
Perfectionists can be a pain

American women expect to find in their husbands a perfection that English women only hope to find in their butlers.

WILLIAM SOMERSET MAUGHAM

Tip

Successful organizations need all types of personalities to make them work.

Getting a job finished, a design completed or a project concluded generally depends on the input of the perfectionist, the master of detail – perhaps even the hyper-fussy. To the extrovert the perfectionist can be excruciating company. The fact is, we need them.

It's when the hyper-fussy becomes the nit-picker, inflexible, rigid and obstinate, that we have a difficult person to deal with. Sticklers for detail often won't realize they are being difficult. From their perspective, detail, rules and regulations are the things that glue organizations together.

They will hide a lack of vision or creativity behind a process, sometimes the law, and always a file of memos and notes.

Why should there be a section in a book about difficult people that is dedicated to perfectionists? In a world of rushing around and doing things half-cocked, shouldn't we try and find a few more perfectionists?

My answer is yes and no! We need the perfectionist's commitment to fine detail and the small print; we can use them to keep us on the straight and narrow. But we can do without the perfectionist's narrow focus, inflexibility and turgid obsession with the rules and regulations. We need to loosen them up a little:

> *'How you deal with all this detail is a mystery. Still, it's a good job someone around here does. But the truth is, on this project we have a tight turnaround time and a lot of effort going into delivery. This time I'm not too worried about the details, we just need to push it along.'*

That might work better than, 'You pedant, can't you see you're holding the whole process up?'

To beat perfectionists at their own game is to commit yourself to perfection. Is what you do as good as it can be? Is it as good as it could be?

There's no point taking on a perfectionist from anywhere but the moral high ground. They might even come to admire you as a kindred spirit.

What motivates a perfectionist

Surprisingly, not the detail, not the books of measurements and the rules. They thrive on a strong sense of accomplishment and achievement. They have high personal standards, which are often their undoing. They are so fixed on getting it right, they lose sight of the big picture. Constantly focusing them on the big picture and the part they play can loosen them a little.

> *'Peter, if you carry on checking the measurements three times/ cross-checking the ledger entries/auditing the software more than once, we'll not only run over budget but we'll miss the delivery date. What can you do to help us?'*

Perfectionists can get lost in their own world and lose all track of time and schedule. Help them with a course on time management. Teach them to break work into sections and set deadlines for each segment. That way they will enhance their sense of achievement, having delivered the goods and to a deadline.

Rules are rules

Every organization has to have rules. Without them there is chaos. However, modern business thrives on origination and spontaneity. Can you be creative within the rules? Yes, you can, but sometimes you have to be creative with the rules.

Soldiers follow the rules and their orders, but most outstanding acts of bravery and courage have taken place against a background of no rules, or the rule book being thrown out of the window. A modern manager is nothing if not creative.

The perfectionist needs to be given permission to be less than perfect:

> *'Peter, you know what we've budgeted for this and I don't want to go any higher. However, we must get delivery on time and with less than 1 per cent quality rejects. If that means we have to sensibly negotiate on the price, so be it. I'll trust your judgement and I know you will use it well.'*

Exercise

Try the priority matrix method next time you are dealing with a perfectionist.

At the outset of a task or project, ask them to commit to the fixed priority for that piece of work: schedule, budget or quality. Circulate the agreement in writing and refer back to it when things appear to be spiralling out of control because of a perfectionist approach.

Think back to a time when a piece of work has been affected by a perfectionist. Would this approach have helped you to keep things on track?

The perfectionist boss

They expect long hours, commitment, blood, sweat and tears. Delegate parts of the job if you can. If it gets too much, say so:

'I know how much store you set by accuracy and delivery, but there is just too much on for me to promise to give either, or perhaps both. Can we talk about breaking the job up or getting some more help?'

Summary points

- Don't try to beat a perfectionist at his or her own game; make them realize that the big picture is sometimes more important and explain why by sticking to the facts.

- To remind perfectionists of the big picture, help them with their understanding of timelines, priorities and what constitutes an acceptable standard.

12
Manipulating the manipulators

Calamities are of two kinds: misfortunes to ourselves, and good fortune to others.

AMBROSE BIERCE

When does management become manipulation? What's the difference between motivation and manipulation? When does manoeuvring become manipulating? The dictionary gives us a clue:

> **manipulate** /məˈnɪpjʊleɪt/ v.tr 1 handle, treat or use, esp. skilfully 2 manage to one's own advantage, esp. unfairly or unscrupulously

In the modern workplace, how can you avoid it? It's dog eat dog out there, but when motivation, management and manoeuvring become unfair we have to do something.

The first rule is, don't try to out-manipulate a manipulator. Instead, deal with it head on. To do otherwise moves you into the complex world of conspiracy, plotting and scheming. Anyway, you haven't got time. Deal with the difficulty and move on.

Being manipulated by the boss? That's tricky. Try this: *'I know you are a fair person, but what you've decided here has caused me a real problem.'* Appealing to their better nature is more likely to pay off than complaining about the manipulation.

If you're being lined up to take the blame

The classic! Your boss, a colleague, even one of your staff, is looking for a fall guy. Hands up who has not come across this scenario.

A project has gone pear shaped and everyone is looking for somewhere to dump the blame. Unfortunately, at the outset of the project, in your normal cheery, optimistic way you said (or worse, wrote in an email) that you thought it looked like a flyer, a great idea. Three months later – crash…

Suddenly, out of a clear blue sky, it was 'your project', 'your fault' and 'down to you'. Ugh! What next?

You could try, *'You're not seriously suggesting all this is down to me, are you?'* Wriggle, squirm!

I doubt that will be enough. Here's a better suggestion:

> *'There were 14 of us involved in this and two main departments. True, it did look OK to me at the outset, but there were a lot of other people involved, including the regional management. Hindsight is a wonderful thing. Perhaps we'd all do better if we stopped laying blame and started building some solutions.'*

That's a much better approach and shows that up with the blame you will not put. Either you all go down, or you all sort it out.

The important thing here is to get this rebuttal up and running fast. That way you avoid being suffocated in the inevitable gossip that surrounds a juicy corporate cock-up.

Lies are manipulations and they don't always come in the big black wriggling form. They can be white lies, half-truths and part of selective omissions. However you wrap it up, if it isn't the truth, the whole truth and nothing but the truth, it's dangerous.

Liars are one step up from manipulators, and it is not a very big step. People who manipulate not just colleagues but the truth as well are easy to deal with. Just stick to the facts, the records, the minutes and the data. Oh, and don't call anyone a liar. As far as you are concerned they are confused, uninformed, not up-to-date and have perhaps taken their eye off the ball. Let the others call them a liar. That way you make allies, not enemies.

Deal with a half-truth as if it was an oversight or an error. The liar will know what you are doing and everyone else will think you're on the ball. *'Lawrence, what you are saying is right, but I think you forgot to mention that the client said they wanted the blue colour in the first batch.'* Avoid being judgemental. *'Lawrence, you left out the client preference from your report. Did you do that to make my department look daft?'* It might be true but it creates friction and aggravation. Just be ready with the facts.

Tip

Difficult situations and difficult people are neutralized by the facts – don't underestimate the importance of keeping notes!

Let's do a deal

This could be the chance of a lifetime, or you could be being manipulated. Your call! You'll have to do the deal to find out. It is a reasonable assumption that the people you are dealing with are honest, but if the deal looks too good to be true, it probably is. Remember, the key to doing a deal is that everyone gets something out of it. Figure out the deal from your side, sure, but more importantly, think about the deal from the other side of the table. What's in it for me? What's in it for them? If it looks like the deal is all on your side, look again!

Verbal promises aren't worth the paper they're not printed on! Manipulators see themselves as deal-makers. If the trade-off involves you promising to do something that is dependent upon someone else doing something, what happens if they don't? Are you stuck, stranded and looking sheepish?

Tip

The first golden rule: if it's right for the project, do it. If in doubt, don't.

The second golden rule: doing deals calls for records, notes and agreements.

Exercise

Review the sample note below:

The purpose of this memo is to record my understanding of what was agreed at the meeting on 31/02/16. John agreed to do this, I agreed to do that, and the whole thing will be delivered by...

Think about some situations where a written record like this could have helped you. Use the following template to start recording business decisions.

Date (time if appropriate)	
Meeting/event details	
Outcome	[Who] agreed to [what]
Outcome	[Who] agreed to [what]
Outcome	[Who] agreed to [what]
Dates/deliverables agreed	
Notes	

> **Tip**
>
> If you are able to circulate notes, do so. Invite others to add to them if they feel anything is recorded incorrectly.

If you're easily flattered

You gorgeous creature! Of course you are. We all are! Ever heard anything like this: 'You are so good at PowerPoint slides, would you make a set for my presentation tomorrow?' And there you are, up until the small hours creating a masterpiece. Manipulated by a master. You should have tried:

> *'Mary, thank you for your kind words, but I find giving a presentation is a personal thing, and you'll be more confident and give a better presentation if you compose the slide-show yourself. If you want to run them by me when you've finished, I'd be happy to help out with the finishing touches.'*

Now you can spend the evening doing what you want to do. If you think you're being manipulated or bounced, you probably are. Good manipulators will go to any length to disguise what they do in flattery and compliments. Trust your instincts. If it doesn't feel right, don't wear it. Dig a bit deeper and ask some questions. Why, when, who, what and where are a few starters.

If you're flattered by your staff

You know you are the dream boss, and once in a while it's nice to be told that you are. But beware of flatterers who use their charms to get you to give them the easy jobs or to overlook their short-comings. Try, *'Sylvia, thank you. It's nice to be appreciated but I think we should get on with the job.'*

Flattery, sycophancy, boot-licking, toadyism: none of it is very nice and you can do without most of it. Beware too of the personal undertones that might accompany flattery. Workplace problems include accusations of inappropriate behaviour and falling foul of the 'politically correct' police. If it looks like there could be a problem, confide in your boss. If you are the boss, talk to a senior member of staff or a lawyer.

Summary points

- Don't engage with manipulators by trying your hand at manipulation yourself – be upfront about everything.

- Lying is a form of manipulation. When faced with a liar, don't call them out on it – instead assume they don't have the full facts. Always have the full facts recorded and documented so you can rebuff their arguments in a non-aggressive way.

- When making deals with manipulators, always analyse what's in it for them. If the deal seems to be only in your favour and is too good to be true, then it probably is.

- Manipulators often use flattery to get what they want. Always investigate their real motives and stick to the job.

13
Morale, attitude and how was it for you?

If you feel depressed you should not go out – because it will show on your face. Misery is a communicable disease.

MARTHA GRAHAM

My starting point for this section is that there is only one person who can affect my morale, and that person is me.

I guess everyone is not like me, and a good thing too, I hear you say! In the real world, the workplace, your organization, there will be pressures, changes and events that will impact on people's attitude to work. Corporate morale is a difficult thing to judge. We are told morale is at rock bottom in public services, yet I can introduce you to inspired teachers, devoted nurses and brilliant doctors. How do you measure morale, and how do you know when it is on the downward run? Use the following exercise to help you look for the signs.

Exercise

Answer the following questions, to help assess how if you could have a morale issue within your team.

- Have you noted regular flash-points and arguments between staff?

- Have sickness and unplanned absence levels risen?

- Have cliques and informal groups appeared?

- Is gossiping rife and are rumours spreading?

If you have answered yes to one or more of these questions, you could have a problem with morale.

What to do?

Chapter 8 deals with flashpoints and anger. Rows and arguments that result from poor morale have to be dealt with in the same basic way, but there is a subtlety. Dealing with a normal row means finding out what the causes of the problem are and dealing with the row and the causes.

Disputes that arise out of poor morale follow the same rules, but the cause of the row is often much more difficult to ferret out.

When someone is having a screaming match try the process outlined in Figure 13.1.

You have to listen! Ask more questions and listen again. At the bottom of the anger, you'll find the reason: gossip about redundancies, changes in working practices making the job more difficult to do, the need for more modern equipment, unexpected workload. It will be there somewhere.

If you're sick of the sick

An otherwise healthy staff member who suddenly starts to have a poor sickness record is a sure sign something is wrong. Whatever is wrong might not be put right in the doctor's surgery. Some telltale signs are absences either side of a weekend or public holiday. Friday and Monday absences, linked with claims of sickness, are worth looking out for.

Figure 13.1 Dealing with a row

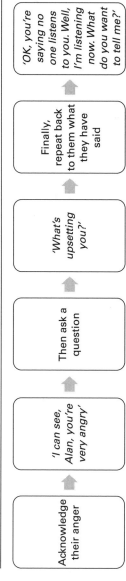

Acknowledge their anger

'I can see, Alan, you're very angry'

Then ask a question

'What's upsetting you?'

Finally, repeat back to them what they have said

'OK, you're saying no one listens to you. Well, I'm listening now. What do you want to tell me?'

Poor morale, lack of motivation, listless performance and a poor sickness record go hand in hand.

Action? Confront the sickness without being intrusive:

'Sheila, I've noticed you've had [number of days] off with sickness in the last quarter/month. I'm concerned about you. Are you a bit 'under the weather' or is there something wrong that I can help you with?'

Tip

Bringing the sickness record to attention is often enough to change a pattern of behaviour.

Do you have access to occupational health services? If you do, you can refer an employee with a sudden decline in healthy days for an opinion. However, don't expect the doctor or nurse to reveal the details of an employee's health: that's confidential. And don't expect the clinicians to do the manager's job of getting a lead-swinger back to work. They can tell you that a member of staff is generally healthy enough to do the job they are hired to do, and they will help an employee with any health problems they come across. That's all.

Everyone having a sickie

Poor morale can lead to endemic lead-swinging. Departments become unmanageable because everyone is using sickness as a way of forgetting their problems at the office.

Exercise

The following tool can be used to measure sickness. Record sickness for a period of no less than a month and not more than a quarter.

	Name	Name	Name	Name	Name	Name	Name	Name
Sick days either side of a bank holiday *– 12 points*								
Sick days either side of a weekend *– 10 points*								
Single sick days during the week *– 8 points*								
Linked mid-week sick days *– 2 points per day*								
Days off for long-term sickness *– 1 point per week*								

This weighted method of scoring highlights the obvious skivers and does not penalize those who are genuinely ill.

You will need to think carefully about how to share the results with your line manager or human resources. This should be in line with company policy. Expect the following to happen:

- Demonstrating that the issue has management attention will impact on the lead-swingers and reduce sickness absences immediately.

- Departments with a high score will probably be the poor performers and will be impacting on other departments. Expect peer pressure to leverage down unacceptable and unwarranted absence levels.

Honestly, or your money back!

Cliques

Organizations with poor morale are often infested by little groups who put themselves 'outside' the organization, in the sense that they look to each other for mutual support and become semi-detached.

They sit, grumbling and festering and conspiring! Just what a paranoid manager needs. They are often the source of gossip. What they don't know, they make up.

Exercise

You can use gossip creatively. If you've got some good news to spread, whisper it, in confidence, to the company gossip. Stand back and wait for it to be spread!

There are two approaches. The first is to break the groups up, moving personnel to other parts of the organization, changing working hours, or changing the work clique members so that they are disconnected from each other. That may not be a practical solution. It is disruptive and may exacerbate an existing morale problem.

The second solution is more Machiavellian. Try giving selected members of the group specific and special tasks for which they must report to you. Encourage them and praise them. Get them onside. In effect, create a positive clique around you. Exploit their talents, reward them with public praise and lift them out of their introspection.

Summary points

- A dip in morale will affect conflicts immediately because often it introduces even more emotions and a lack of reasoning to the situation.

- A lack of morale will often bring with it a rise in sick days being taken – when dealing with people who take an unreasonable amount of sick days, always bring it up and question it with them directly first.

- Don't let groups of disgruntled and unmotivated employees fester. Make sure you engage with the individuals within the group and limit the opportunities for them to get together and complain.

14
Fault-finders and nit-pickers

There is absolutely nothing wrong with [him] that a miracle can't fix.

ALEXANDER WOOLLCOTT

How do you deal with a fault-finder? Answer – don't have any faults! If only it were that easy. When staff take a pride in what they do, a grudging fault-finder rumbling away in the corner can be a real downer.

You really do have to nip their unwelcome interventions in the bud.

'Fiona, I want you to remember the whole department has put a huge amount of effort into this. I think a lot of them feel your constant fault-finding is pretty hard to take. I want you to make a list of all the things that you see as wrong and go though it with me. Let's get the criticisms dealt with and out of the way.'

You could try getting them to acknowledge what is good and help out, getting the rest out of the way:

'Fred, I know this isn't perfect but we have managed to eliminate 90 per cent of the quality errors and guarantee claims. What do you think we should be doing to go to the next step?'

Creative fault-finders? Is there such a thing? Sure. Use them. They are often the masters of detail and they can be harnessed to use their talents more creatively: *'I know you're very critical of this project, Christine, and you've found a number of faults in it. I want you to have a good look at the programme before we submit it and point out anything else you think may not be right.'*

If you have a nit-picker for a boss

To deal with generalized criticism of the 'This just won't do' variety, ask the boss to be specific. *'I hear your opinion that you're not happy with what I've done, but for me to put it right I need you to be more specific.'*

Invite criticism and try to stay clear of opinion. Focus on the specifics of what is wrong, and get the boss to see it in the context of the totality of the work. It can't be all bad, can it?

A sarcastic boss? Ugly. Sarcasm, the lowest form of wit? So they say. Don't treat it as wit. Don't laugh when the boss says of a colleague 'Look at her trying to be the customer relations department!'

In reply, say, *'I think Mary does very well with the customers, she tries really hard to please them. Anyway, where would we all be without customers?'*

Nit-picking colleagues

Sitting next to fault-finders makes the working day seem longer. The trick is not to shun them or ignore them. The right approach is to get really close to them. Ask for their opinions as often as you can.

> **Tip**
>
> If colleagues moan and pick holes, ask them questions. Dig deep into their opinions, and demand they back up opinion with fact. I bet they won't have too many facts!

The more you dig, the less often they will find fault. Fault-finders often do their dirty work without much thought. It becomes a habit, a mindset and superficial. By questioning them, you make them think. That requires effort and they will soon pack it in.

On the positive side, by digging you might find the seeds of useful criticism that you can put to work, to improve what you are doing.

Staff who find fault, whine and grumble can be teased out of their mindset by getting them involved in solving the problem they are whinging about. 'The car park lighting is useless' deserves, '*Lucinda, I was thinking the same thing myself. I want you to look into the practicality and costs of upgrading it. Would you let me have some proposals by the end of next week?*' This approach occupies the fault-finder, shuts them up for a while, makes them feel important and gets the car park lights sorted!

> If you are a positive-minded soul, you will probably try to shut out the fault-finders of this world. Try another way: '*Karl, I really appreciate what you've said about this work. I've taken on board what you said and I think you've helped me to do a better job.*' See, now you've got a fan!

Exercise

Think back to a time when you have encountered somebody fault-finding. Would any of the approaches suggested above have altered the situation? How?

Summary points

- Deal with fault-finders immediately and don't let them bring others down. Ask them to help with the project and empower them where possible to fix what they think is wrong.

- If you're dealing with a boss that is a fault-finder, always ask for very specific feedback on what is not good enough in your work. That way, you can deal with each individual issue head on and you're forcing them to back up their criticism with facts.

- You can use fault-finding colleagues to your advantage: involve them as often as possible and really dig deep into their criticism. It might unveil some worthy issues, but most of the time they will back down.

15
Gossip: a bush fire you can do without

There are many who dare not kill themselves, for fear of what the neighbours will say.

CYRIL CONNOLLY

Gossip has to be one of the most corrosive influences on corporate culture. It has two sources.

The first is careless talk. Maybe some major change is in the offing. Perhaps something is going to impact on the organization. People will be tense and uneasy. They will be looking for clues about their future. A careless word, a conversation overheard in a lift, the car park or the canteen, can start a hare running. This kind of thing happens. It is avoidable, and good management, timely communications and a commitment to openness can stop gossip dead in its tracks. That is a management issue, and there are management techniques to ensure that gossip is not given a chance.

The second type of gossip is probably the more damaging. It is the gossip that is started by people who don't have any facts. There are no fragments of information that they are trying to piece together. This is the sort of gossip that is started by the uninformed, the disenfranchised and the downright dim.

Was there ever a truer phrase than 'knowledge is power'? There are people in organizations who, in order to make themselves

Figure 15.1 Map of a bush fire – how gossip lights up your day!

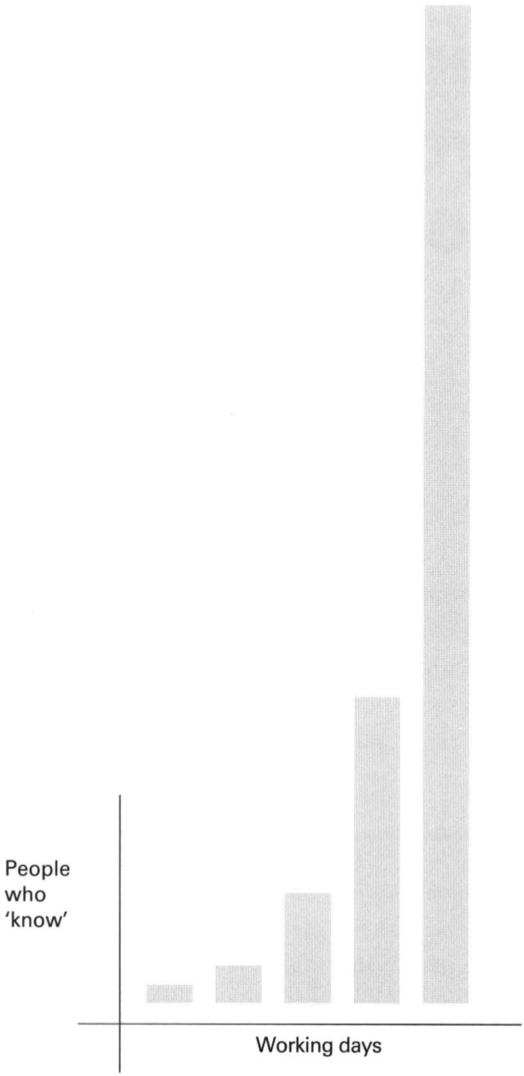
People
who
'know'
Working days

appear powerful, will create gossip and rumour. They want to make it look like they are 'in the know'. They can do the most enormous damage.

Of the few studies done around the organizational dynamics of gossip, one of the most telling was carried out by Anders Vidners, now a professor at Stockholm University but previously a corporate guru who worked with the Swedish pharmaceutical giant Astra (later to become the subject of a corporate merger and turn into AstraZeneca). Vidners showed that in large organizations one person could have a 'meaningful dialogue' with 15 other people during the course of an ordinary working day. Here's how gossip spreads; $15 \times 15 \times 15$. Figure 15.1 makes it even clearer.

Spooky, isn't it? One person talking to 15 is bad enough. Fifteen talking to another 15 gets worrying: it means 225 people may have the wrong message. After that, the sums get silly: $225 \times 15 = 3,375$. Soon enough the whole world has got hold of the wrong end of the stick.

The more the message is spread, the less accurate it gets. Gossip is like a bush fire. It starts as a spark and turns itself into a forest fire. It is almost impossible to stop and before you know it there's nothing left.

Figure 15.2 As a message is spread, it can get more and more inaccurate

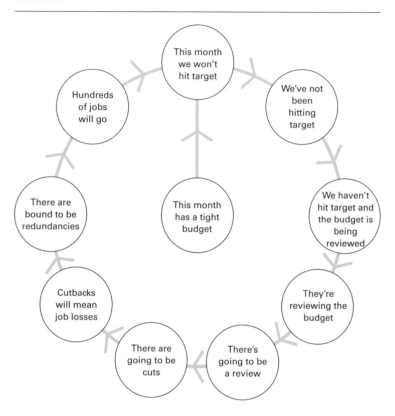

The answer to gossip problems

Rumour-mongers are immature, and the only real answer isn't always pleasant. You have to confront them. *'Harry, I need to ask you something. Did you say [repeat the rumour]; is that right?'* Expect an answer along the lines of. 'Well it must be, because...'. Don't expect the culprit to own up. That's for the grown-ups!

Confronting the gossip is not enough by itself. You run the risk of them saying, 'It must be true, they tried to shut me up.' The trick is to confront the gossip and put the record straight at the same time. '*Harry, what you are saying isn't true. The facts are…*'. So to confront the gossip, you need to have the facts.

Sometimes there will be sensitive issues that you can't deal with right away. In that case, try this:

> '*Harry, what you are saying isn't true. There are very good reasons why, at the moment, it isn't possible to say anything about the issue, but we expect to be able to make a statement in the next 24 hours. My advice to you is to wait until you have all the facts before you say any more.*'

The next step is to be sure you make the statement on time. If you don't, you will be rewarded with more gossip!

Tip

Don't think, for one moment, this is just a big company problem. Small organizations are just as prone to being burned by gossip. Small companies have customers, suppliers and associates. Gossip spreads inside and outside the organization and can do some real damage to credibility and reputation.

Prevention is better than cure

Gossip can easily get out of hand and can be the devil's own job to eradicate. A good communications strategy is the answer. The sorts of issues that are likely to worry staff and get tongues wagging are easy to spot. Use the exercise below to prepare some positive communications on some typical gossip triggers.

Exercise

Spend some time thinking about how you could share positive communications on the following themes. These are typical gossip-inducing events. Use the structure below to help you to share the news but end with a positive note. Use the first example as a guide.

Event	Why it happened	Impact	Moving forward
Poor results	The closing down sales from our main competitor took away spend from customers that we would have expected to spend more with us this quarter	We didn't make as many sales as we would expect for this time of year	Now that the competitor has closed, we can expect to see that custom come back and next quarter's results should balance out the loss, or even be higher than typically expected
The loss of a big order			
A potential take-over			
A key member of staff leaving			
A change of major supplier			
Moving premises			

Letting people know what is going on stops gossip dead in its tracks.

Corporate politics, sensitive negotiations, delicate issues can't always be brought into the public domain. Remember, because you can't speak doesn't mean others won't.

What's the answer? Easy: say you can't say anything.

'I know there has been some rumour about [whatever the issue is]. I'm anxious to put an end to the gossip. I can't say anything right now but I will be able to give some hard information on [name a sensible timescale].'

Be sure you follow through on the promise, otherwise expect some more problems with gossip.

Summary points

- Gossip spreads extremely quickly and usually starts with casual conversations being inadequately relayed or with people who are disenfranchised and don't stick to the truth. Deal with it quickly so the problem doesn't get out of hand.

- The easiest way to deal with a gossiper is to confront them and correct their statements at the same time. Make them stick to the facts and very soon they won't be able to back up their statements.

- You can also pre-empt gossip from flaring up by making sure your teams have the right level of information at all times.

16

The customer is always right – really?

All English shop assistants are Miltonists. All Miltonists firmly believe that 'they also serve who only stand and wait'.

GEORGE MIKES

The customer is always right? Er, actually, no. Well, I mean, yes. If you see what I mean!

Customers can be a real pain: demanding, difficult and downright belligerent. But they are also the clothes on your back, the roof over your head and the shoes on your feet.

The world has moved on. There was a time when customers would put up with second-best, accept excuses and be reluctant to complain. Not any more. In this consumer driven, 24–7–365 economy, if you don't deliver, there is plenty of choice and customers will move on. Sometimes customers will push to the point where you have to make some serious decisions about just how far you will and can afford to go. It's better to bring the relationship to an end in a civilized way than have it ended, for you, in a blazing row.

Customers don't always get it right. They complain when they really have no right to complain, they exaggerate, lie and can be a crooked as a Great Train Robber. Laws protecting customers are abused and lawyers exploiting their no-win–no-fee new-found freedoms are probably another aggravation you can do without. Grim, isn't it? But the customer is always right!

The real trick is not to have difficult customers! Deliver what and when you say you will, give value for money and be ready to act fast if something does go wrong, and you needn't read this section. If, on the other hand, you live in the real world, you might want to glance at it!

Dealing with difficult customers

No apologies for the over-use of the next word: communication. It is at the heart of good staff relations and it is at the heart of good customer/client relations. It is of course a two-way thing. To communicate, you've got to get the customer's attention and be sure you understand what they are asking for. Not sure the customer is paying attention, or they are unclear in what they want? Try this. *'I just want to make sure I've understood you correctly. To get this right, you will want…'* (Then describe what they are demanding.) This has the dual effect of clarifying the situation and, by playing back what they said, makes outrageous demands seem silly, even to those who made them!

Once clarified, translate it into an order, a specification or a record.

You want it when?

What about the really demanding customer? Offer less and do more, that's the key! Be sure not to get it the other way around.

As always, it's in the words:

'Oh, that's a tall order. You're setting us a real challenge here because we don't usually turn an order around in that time/ make it in that colour/get the paperwork through the system in that timescale, but we'll do our best.'

By setting up the anticipation that you might not be able to deliver, when you do, you'll have one delighted customer. If you don't, you've created some room for manoeuvre.

Exercise

Something gone really wrong? Go to visit the client. Even if you never normally visit, do it. Show the client they are worth the journey, the time and the cost. Look them in the eyes, read their body language and say, *'We messed this up and I'm here to say sorry and to find out how we can put it right.'*

Avoiding trouble

Get it in writing. Tedious? Yes, but a well-written contract has dug many folk out of a difficult situation. Don't think it has to be something like the Maastricht Treaty. A simple note of who is going to do what, when and at what price is all that's needed.

Defining accountability and expectations is simple good practice. From time to time, everyone has a fallible memory. Later on, if there is a problem, you have the opportunity to say, *'I've looked at the agreement we had and it seems pretty clear to me, you agreed we should [whatever the task or service was]. I think you'll agree with me, that's exactly what we have done.'*

The really, really, really, really difficult customer

Try a chaperone. Appoint someone with special responsibility to look after a valued but difficult customer. Give the customer a reference point, easy access, a direct phone number and a named person. Sit back and watch the complaints fall. Many times complaints fester and get worse because they are not dealt with expeditiously, or the process of having a moan turns a disappointed customer into a difficult customer. Make it easy for someone to be difficult, and they won't be. Honestly – or your money back!

How do they run their ship? A really good guide to what prospective clients or customers might expect from you is how they run their business. If everything is lined up, shipshape, neat and tidy, that's your signal not to be sloppy. If they have a reputation for looking after their customers, delivering on time and offering terrific value, you know what you've got to do!

Remind them how good you are

Giving great value for money and stunning service? Tell your customers, remind them and then tell them again. How? Spell it out on an invoice. Step by step, itemize the components of what you are charging for. Avoid wording such as:

To:

Attend and repair Model Z134

Total: £250 + VAT

Use the invoice as an advertisement. Try:

To:

Attend within 3 hrs of call out request + locate problem in Model Z134 using diagnostic equipment + carry out repair using replacement component from stock on service van + reassemble + clean and service generally + unit back in service within 45 minutes of attending.

Total: £250 + VAT

I know which invoice I'd feel better about paying.

The screamer

Don't you just love a good scream? Babies do it all the time, just to get your attention. And we know it works. Screamers come in all shapes and sizes. They can be customers, colleagues, the boss, the neighbour, even family. The solution is the same for all of them. Here's what you do:

Take a copy of this book and hit them on the head with it.

No, no, no! As much as you may want to do it, resist the temptation. First rule with a screamer is don't join in. Don't get into a decibel competition. Screamers are juvenile and wouldn't do it if they could see how silly they look.

They want attention, so give it to them. Listen, let them scream. Let the accusations, the smears, the insinuations, the abuse and rudeness fly over your head. Let them have a good blast. When they tire and stop for breath, pick your moment. Step in and say something.

The important thing here is to pick your moment. You won't silence a screamer, but you can wait until they run out of steam. So judge the moment and say, *'Can we get to what's really wrong here? Help me understand...'* (go to the issues). It may not work the first time. Let the next instalment of invective pass you by and try again. Keep going, because it is the only way.

> One way to bring screamers down off the ceiling is to speak in a voice that is just a touch quieter than you would normally use. That way they have to pay attention and listen.

On the phone

No matter how bad it gets, never hang up. If you do, you have two problems to deal with: the whatever-it-was they were screaming about in the first place AND getting over the fact you slammed the phone down.

You can get off the line by saying, *'I'm going to have to go now but I'll call you back in just two minutes.'* Don't do this to duck out of trouble – be sure to ring back. The chances are when you do ring back they will have calmed down. Well, that's the theory! It usually works – but no money back if it doesn't! Just stay calm.

Tip

Never deal with a screamer on the phone, sitting down. Stand up and the tone and texture of your voice will change. You can 'hear' body language. You'll sound more interested. Honestly!

In public

If the screamer is in public, you'll probably want to get them into a quieter, more private environment. Use the right words and some body language. Say, *'OK, I think I understand, let's get to the bottom of it. Can we go to my office so that I can make some notes.'*

The next thing is the behaviour changer: the body language bit. Turn half away, gesture in the general direction of the office and take half a step but keep eye contact.

If you've judged it right, the screamer will follow you. If not, let them scream a bit longer and say the same again.

Some people-management gurus will tell you to deal with a screamer by saying things like, 'I'm not going to carry on with this if you shout at me' or 'Please don't use that language to me' or 'Please try to behave in a more mature fashion'.

The grim news is it will make the situation worse. There is no excuse for bad language and aggression, but highlighting it will simply ignite more trouble and invite another load of air.

Just stay cool and let it pass you by.

If a member of your staff blows a gasket

They just lose it. Like a volcano, whoosh! If they are a member of staff you want to keep, life after a good scream will be difficult, but it can be managed.

Although you'll have to make it clear that 'that sort of behaviour' is not on, during the incident is not the time. Don't embarrass them. They will be embarrassed enough when it is over. Don't make it worse. Manoeuvre the person into a quiet place and say, *'We need to sort this out. I'm going to leave you for a couple of minutes to collect your thoughts, then I'll come back and we'll go through it together.'*

Afterwards, insist that the individual apologizes to anyone who was in earshot. It doesn't have to be a heavy, sackcloth and ashes apology. *'I think you do owe them an apology and to clear the air with them, don't you?'*

Every once in a while even the best member of staff will have a funny five minutes and blow their stack.

The trick is to make the path back to normality as easy as possible.

> **Tip**
>
> Avoid recriminations or referring to the incident once it has been dealt with. Move on.

When the screamer is the boss

Everyone ducks – that's what happens! The boss does have the power of the boot. Now is not the time to challenge them to use it. As with all screamers, the golden rule is to let them scream. It is the platinum, diamond-encrusted rule when the screamer is the boss. Ride out the storm, let it flow over you and under no circumstances scream back.

After the storm cometh the quiet. Pick your moment and say, *'I know you are very cross but the whole incident was embarrassing for everyone. Can we please find some time to go through exactly what you want?'*

Tip

Chances are, when anyone blows their stack, there'll be a hidden reason, not just work-related. Is it anything you can help with?

Dealing with very rude people without being very rude

Quite often, people are rude without knowing they are being rude. They are what workplace shrinks call overly focused.

They'll jump all over your conversations, interrupt, finish off your sentences and monopolize the discussion. Ever thought about why they do it? Quite often rudeness has its roots in shyness and a feeling of inadequacy.

That rude person who jumps into your conversation probably doesn't look very shy, but inside them there is a little voice that says, 'If I don't jump in, I'll never get my point across.' Seeing the rude person in that context makes them more a person to feel sorry for than to get excited about.

The professional rude person will monopolize a conversation and make it impossible for anyone else to get a word in edgeways.

Let them ramble on. Sooner or later they will drift away from the subject in hand. Pick your moment, and break in with, *'This is all very interesting but what has it got to do with the agenda item?*

Shouldn't we focus on...?' Use that as a way of getting yourself and others back into the conversation. Don't think you'll be on your own. In a group meeting the others will recognize their time has come and support you.

Tip

The classic, 24-carat, copper-bottomed, 100-per-cent rude person is verging on being a bully. Bullies need a victim, so don't be a victim.

Walk away politely and come back later. That will defuse the tension and send a signal that you will not put up with that!

Disguised rudeness

The classic example of this has to be the back-handed compliment, or the put-down.

You know the sort of thing: 'Good sales figures, Brian, but I guess they're not real sales. Most of them were from government procurement anxious to spend their budgets by the end of the financial year?'

Don't put up with it! Have some sense of self worth. *'Thanks, I worked hard on them. What do you mean by "not real sales"?'* Watch them back off.

Summary points

- Good communication is at the heart of dealing with difficult customers. Make sure you understand the level of service or the product they are after and on the other hand give them a full understanding of what you can offer them.

- Always build in contingency plans and give yourself more time so that you don't over-promise and under-deliver. Instead, surprise them with an earlier positive outcome.

- If you can, always get everything agreed in writing.

- Don't get into a screaming match with a customer. Always defuse the situation and wait until you can reason with them, in private.

- Rudeness can also be defused. Ask difficult, rude people to clarify their position and that will force them to reframe the conversation or back down.

17
Complaints: we love them

Six steps to success

Got a screamer? Ouch! Won't let you get a word in edgeways? Here's the fail-safe technique for dealing with a complaint:

Figure 17.1   A process for dealing with a complaint

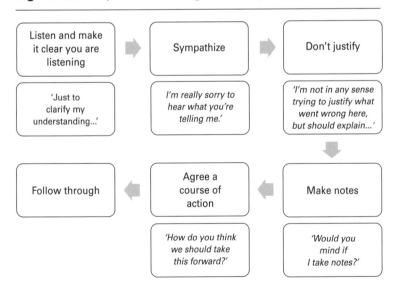

Let's take it step by step.

Listen

Here's the trick: listen and let the other person know you are listening. Use body language and physical prompts to show you're listening.

It costs nothing to listen, and the more attentive you are, the more you will defuse the situation. Pay attention to what the complainant is saying, concentrate and ask questions: *'Just to clarify my understanding'* or *'This sounds terrible, would you just tell me that bit again?'*

Sympathize

Sympathizing is not the same as agreeing, it doesn't mean accepting liability and it doesn't signal that you have surrendered. What it does do is to help to take the heat out of the situation. A few well-chosen words reaffirm you are listening and you are not trying to duck out of the situation.

Here are a few well-chosen words:

- *'I'm really sorry to hear what you're telling me.'*
- *'That sounds awful to me.'*
- *'That must have been very difficult for you.'*

Don't justify

The irate person in front of you is not in the least bit interested in the fact that half the staff are off work with the flu, the delivery you were expecting hasn't showed, the boss is on your back for more sales, you crashed the car on the way to work, the youngest cried all night and you had a row with the other half.

It's not their problem.

Whatever the reason, whatever the problem, now is not the time to bring it up.

There will be a time, later, to explain why things have apparently gone wrong. But in the life of the complaint, now is not the time. It is too early. At the right time, it is OK to say:

'I'm not in any sense trying to justify what went wrong here, but you do need to know, we've had a fire in the warehouse and all our deliveries are behind. I know your delivery is urgent and I will go and see what I can do to bring it forward.'

Tip

Don't say things like:

- *'I can't believe it.'*
- *'You're putting me on.'*
- *'This can't be true.'*
- *'You're joking.'*
- *'What? No, surely not!'*

Even if you don't believe it, there's no point in making a bad situation worse by calling a complainer a liar, or hinting you think they are. The objective here is to defuse the situation, deal with the complaint with the minimum collateral damage and get on with your life.

Make notes

There is something reassuring about having someone write down your complaint.

What we are talking about here is making a simple record of who is complaining, when and what it's about. Why? First, it reinforces the listening message, and second, notes made contemporaneously might be a godsend if everything gets out of hand later on.

A summary of the complaint, made at the time, is usually a reliable record of what happened and is made before the complainant has had time to embroider the problem or fester in the compost heap of compensation.

Agree a course of action

OK, what are you going to do next? You've listened, sympathized, made notes. What's next? Agree a course of action. How? Ask:

- *'How do you think we should take this forward?'*
- *'How would you like me to handle this from here?'*
- *'How do you see resolving the situation?'*

By asking these types of questions you will get a feel for how far you will need to go to get this out of your in-tray. It doesn't mean you're capitulating or ready to roll over. It just gives you a sense of what it might take to resolve the issue.

Maybe what the complainant asks for is reasonable, within your responsibility to grant and you can deliver. In which case – job done.

On the other hand, it might be they are asking too much, it is outside your remit or the whole thing is starting to look like a put-up job. In this case a few more well-chosen words are called for:

- *'I know you will want me to get to the bottom of this, so I'm going to ask you to give me a couple of hours/days to look into this properly.'*
- *'I can't authorize what you are asking for, so I am going to take this matter to the manager and ask them to help.'*
- *'There are several people involved in this matter and I am going to have to ask you to give me some time to sort it out.'*
- *'This seems very serious to me and I know you wouldn't want anyone else to have to go through it. I'll need time to make proper enquiries.'*

The next segment in handling a complaint is the pivotal bit. Without this, all the rest of the action has been a waste of time.

Follow through

In other words, deliver what you promised. If you agree to call someone back 'this afternoon, when I have made enquiries', be sure to do it. No news yet? No information to hand? No matter. Call back and say, *'I know I promised I'd call you this afternoon, once I had made enquiries. Unfortunately, the person I need to speak to has been away from the building all day. He'll be back here tomorrow and I will speak to him and call you by lunchtime.'* If there is still no news, do the same thing again. Keep doing it until you have a resolution.

Promised to mail a new part, extra thingamajig, or post a replacement widget? Do it, or call and say why you couldn't do it and agree another deadline. Follow-through is the most important stage in dealing with complaints.

Tip

The easiest way to make a bad situation worse is failing to follow through. Telephone call, letter, email: whatever it is, do it. Even if you can't deliver what you thought you could, call back and say so. Agree another deadline.

So, what have we got? It sounds something like this:

'Mrs Bloggs, I need to listen to what you're saying properly. Can we move into my office so that I can make a note of what you are telling me?

Oh dear, this sounds like we have let you down/this is a big disappointment/you must be very upset with us.

> *Let me make a proper note of what you are telling me. Could you just tell me that bit again?*
>
> *I'm not able to authorize what you are asking me to do. However, my supervisor/boss, the MD, will be here this afternoon and I will ask for their help. I'll call you back before the close of business.'*

Be sure you do call back.

If you hear yourself sounding like this, read the previous few pages again:

> *'I can't believe we got it this wrong. The problem is we've got three staff off with the flu and we're really behind in our order section. I'm not sure when I can sort this out. By the way, what did you say your name was?'*

Once in a while, in every organization, mistakes will occur. It is no great sin to get things wrong. It is a sin to get things wrong and not put them right, or to get things wrong too often, or, worst of all, to get things wrong and not know about it.

Tip

The trick is to learn from mistakes and near-misses.

Organizations that encourage an openness about complaints, staff foul-ups and mistakes learn about their systems, protocols and approaches. Mistakes and complaints cost time and money, but they are also an opportunity.

Tip

Handled correctly, a complaining customer can become an advocate and a champion.

Audit complaints, analyse them and use them as a stepping stone to better performance. Don't let them become a millstone.

Exercise

Imagine a customer complaint, or think back to a complaint that you have received in the past. Use the process we looked at earlier to work through a response.

Listen:

Sympathize:

Don't justify:

Make notes:

Agree a course of action:

Follow through:

Summary point

- There are six steps to dealing with complaints: listen to the complaint, sympathize with the person, don't justify or make excuses, make notes, agree a course of action with the complainer and always follow through with the agreed course of action.

18
e-difficult@ yourplace

Having a laugh, innocent fun, office jokes. You must be used to them by now. Once the jokes were told around the tea trolley or in the canteen. Then it was the funny cartoons copied on the new Xerox machine. Now there is email, instant messenger, etc.

This is much more difficult to deal with. The office jokers have a new toy. More importantly, it is not just the office joker. It's the office jokers in all the other offices, far and wide, who can dump their stuff into your system.

Smutty jokes, lewd pictures, unacceptable stories whiz around the email systems and get circulated indiscriminately. Litigation, writs and battles are just an email away. The problems will start internally, then the outside world will come crashing down on the heads of unsuspecting management.

Unless you get a grip on the office jokers, racists and the smutty minded, expect problems. Difficult lawsuits alleging every-thing from sexual discrimination to breach of confidence have been sparked by companies without proper email policies and planning.

Tip

Email policies are fundamental to the way good organizations run their affairs.

Emails can easily be faked or fiddled with and printed-out messages can be similarly counterfeited. In some systems, planting a blank email into a file history makes it possible at a later stage to go back and fill it in with any message you like. This is a trick likely to fool everyone, even an experienced observer.

A storage system that is tamper-proof does not come cheap and will eat up a storage disc faster than an American termite can chomp its way through a house.

If you've found someone circulating bad taste emails, try this:

'Fred, I know you think this kind of thing is funny, and to some people perhaps it is. But there are some others who will be offended, and I cannot risk the company, its reputation and the chance of a lawsuit or tribunal. I'm telling you it has to stop, and if it happens again there will be a formal warning and you risk disciplinary action.'

Here are six ideas to avoid e-fail with email:

	Check ✓
• Warn all staff with an 'on-screen' message about the organization's rules for email. Use the screen saver to do it at zero cost.	
• Make it clear that email is not confidential and will be routinely monitored. More importantly, hammer home the fact that email is not a substitute for the kind of conversation that used to take place in the canteen, lavatory or lift.	
• Stamp out digital gossip; bar the transmission of personal mail, jokes, smutty material and non-business messages.	
• Set up in-house e-training to help staff understand the rules. This might persuade a court that you have taken your responsibilities seriously. Incorporate email policies into contracts of employment.	
• Install a program to monitor email for key words and phrases to flag up offensive material.	

	Check ✓
• Decide on archive policies now: what to keep, how long to keep it, how to keep it and who is responsible. Cost electronic archive processes and budget for it – the outlay is more than you think.	

Exercise

Create your own email checklist and circulate to your staff. If you can, hold a meeting to make sure everyone understands the content of the checklist and to invite questions. An open discussion about e-difficulties could be very valuable to you and your team.

Summary points

- Emails have the potential to become very problematic. It allows material that is not appropriate for the office to be widely communicated and presents risks of putting your reputation and that of your company in jeopardy.
- Deal with bad email behaviour immediately and instil a proper email policy whilst confronting difficult email users.

19
Social networking

Social networking is a way of life. Electronic gossiping and keeping in touch. What could be simpler? It's become part of our every day.

An email or two, a holiday picture on Facebook, a Tweet – all a bit of fun. That's all, just fun.

Well, it can be fun or it can turn into something far more sinister and worrying.

First, it is important to realize that it is not just your friends who will see what you are up to on Facebook and elsewhere. Increasingly, employers and prospective employers will search the internet before they think about offering you the job to die for or the promotion you've been working for.

An injudicious posting can be the difference between getting the job and getting passed over.

Also, the glimpses of your personal side and a peep behind the curtain of your private life is an invitation for people who've decided they don't like you, are jealous of you, envious or just plain mischievous.

A word to the wise

Exercise

The 'Mother Test'

Don't put anything on your Facebook page, Tweet or make any statement on LinkedIn or any other social media site that you wouldn't be happy for your mother to read!

If there are pictures on any of these sites that make you look anything but dignified and sensible, delete them right now. They may be a snapshot of you having a good time on a Greek Island five years ago but you can bet they will come back and haunt you. There is a time when we all have to grow up!

Don't know how to do it? Try this for Facebook:

1 Go to the photo and select the *Options* menu from menu bar beneath the photo.

2 Click *Delete this photo*.
   Here is the important bit: You won't be able to delete a photo if you didn't upload it. To prevent a photo from appearing on your profile (timeline), click *Hidden from timeline* at the top of the comment box of the photo.

Cyberbullying – what is it?

Cyberbullying is no different from any other bullying:

- *Someone who annoys you and antagonizes you.* A bully is a browbeater who wants to bulldoze you into agreeing or doing something you don't really want to do. Moving up the scale, a bully is: a coercer, harrier, hector and often insolent. And off the scale: a bully is an intimidator, oppressor and persecutor. A bully is a pest and tormenter and usually a coward. People are bullies, usually because, at some stage in their life, they have been bullied and know its power.

- *A cyberbully is no different; they just use technology to do it.* The anonymity that technology creates makes it much easier for bullies to operate. They once had to be a bully face to face or use the mail. Then, the telephone. Now, email, instant messaging, web pages and digital photos make it much easier.

This is a good definition of bullying:

A person is bullied when they are exposed, repeatedly and over time, to negative actions on the part of one or more other persons and they have difficulty defending themselves.

There are three important components:

- Bullying is aggressive behaviour that involves unwanted, negative actions.
- Bullying involves a pattern of behaviour over time.
- Bullying involves an imbalance of power or strength.

Cruel or embarrassing rumours, threats, harassment or even stalking are made much easier at the touch of a button.

Teenagers are especially vulnerable. Bullying has moved from the playground to the screen.

However, it is becoming increasingly common in the workplace and there are now many firms of lawyers who specialize in this work. One such firm, Hodge Halsall, has created a useful list of what bullying might include (it doesn't matter whether it is 'electronic' or not):

- abusive, insulting or offensive language used in emails or even face to face;

- embarrassment, even humiliation through gestures, sarcasm, criticism and insults, sometimes lewd or inappropriate photographs or jokes;
- on the part of the boss or supervisor, setting unrealistic targets or deadlines that are difficult to achieve or tasks that are beyond a person's competency or skill levels;
- undermining or sabotaging a person's work by, perhaps, deliberately withholding or supplying incorrect information, denying access to information or resources or even not passing on messages;
- unjustified criticism, often persistently about petty, irrelevant and insignificant matters;
- offensive messages on email, text or telephone;
- making a person the butt of practical jokes;
- deliberately excluding and isolating a person from workplace activities.

The Andrea Adams Trust, a UK charity dedicated to tackling workplace bullying, says there is no simple definition of bullying because of the variety of forms it can take and the situations in which it can arise but comments that it involves 'a gradual wearing down process that makes individuals feel demeaned and inadequate, that they can never get anything right, and that they are hopeless, not only within their work environment, but also within their domestic life'.

Poor management

Poor workplace management is almost always the root-cause of bullying, no matter whether it is electronic or personal. If bullies think they can get away with it they will. Good management should act promptly and stamp it out.

The workplace arbitrators Acas tell us bullying is most likely to occur where there are poor management skills and inadequate complaints handling procedures to deal with workplace grievances. Acas tell us that bullying may become an issue as a result of:

- an authoritarian style of management;
- failure to address previous incidences of bullying;
- unrealistic targets or deadlines;
- prejudice and discrimination;
- personality of colleagues/managers;
- inappropriate performance management systems.

It's just too easy

It is easy to hide in the undergrowth of the internet. Setting up an anonymous email account is all too easy. A determined, organized bully doesn't have to be a technical boffin to take advantage of the obscurity the internet offers.

Because there is no personal contact bullies, mostly weaklings, find it easier to wreak havoc in people's lives sitting at a computer screen. Whilst they may be invisible when they press the 'Send' button, their work becomes immediately visible to hundreds, maybe thousands and in extreme cases, millions.

The ease with which cyberbullying may be carried out can often embolden a perpetrator towards more serious behaviour.

What can you do to protect yourself from cyberbullying?

- *If you do use social media think very carefully what you post.* Use the 'Mother Test'. By limiting the number of people who know about your activities, lifestyle, habits and preferences it will be more difficult for a bully to pick up enough information to paint a bigger picture and may limit your risk of becoming a victim. Limiting the number of people will also make it easier to identify a bully.

- *Try to avoid making the situation worse.* Escalation is to be avoided at all costs! Depending on how bad the situation is, the best response is no response. Bullies thrive on reaction. They want to know the power they have. Consider changing your personal email address and closing social media sites. It may seem like the bully has won. Not really; it just takes away their target and they are likely to move on. If they follow you to a new address, you have a different kind of problem, an even stronger case for legal action and a chat with the police.

- *Keep a record.* As distressing as it may be and however strong the temptation to 'press Delete', don't. Keep all the evidence. Keep emails in an 'Evidence' file. If it is not possible to download the offensive material into a file, take a 'screenshot'.

Exercise
How to take a screenshot

The 'Print Screen' button may be labelled 'PrtScn', 'PrntScrn', 'PrintScrn', or similar. On most keyboards, the button is usually found next to the 'F12' and 'Scroll Lock' keys. On laptop keyboards, you may have to press the 'Fn' or 'Function' key to access 'Print Screen'. Open Microsoft Paint and select 'Paste', or right click on the canvas and select 'Paste' and the screenshot will appear.

Wherever possible print out a hard copy and include the date and time.

If you are being bullied, REPORT IT – DON'T HIDE IT. Report it to your manager, your manager's manager, the police, your trades union or professional organization's representative. If your workplace has one, report it to your HR department.

You are not alone

In 2005 the Department of Trade and Industry carried out a workplace survey. It was called the Fair Treatment at Work Survey and told us 5 per cent of those interviewed had personally experienced bullying or harassment at work in the previous two years.

More than 1 in 10 said they were aware of another person who had been bullied or harassed within the same time period.

What does the law tell us?

It is law that employers have to have a minimum procedure for resolving grievances (electronic or not). The Employment Act 2002 (Dispute Resolution) Regulations 2004 and subsequent review in 2008, established a three step standard grievance procedure:

Step 1 The employee must set out the grievance in writing and send it to the employer.

Step 2 The employer must invite the employee to attend a meeting to discuss the grievance and after the meeting must inform the employee of the decision taken in response to the grievance and of the right to appeal against that decision.

Step 3 If the employee informs the employer they wish to appeal the employer must invite the employee to attend an appeal meeting following which the employer must inform the employee of the final decision.

A modified procedure for pursuing grievances exists in certain circumstances where the employment has already ended.

All employers should have an anti-bullying policy with clear guidelines. The checklist below will help you to evaluate whether or not you have an adequate policy.

Checklist

- Does the employer provide a commitment to foster a bullying free workplace?

- Does the employer confirm that bullying will not be tolerated and detail the consequences of breaking company standards?

- Does the employer describe which kinds of behaviour are acceptable and which are not?

- Does the employer indicate where and how victims can get help?

- Does the employer make a clear commitment to no retaliation against employees who report workplace bullying?

- Does the employer outline the disciplinary action that will be taken against those who are alleged to have bullied or victimized someone who has made a complaint or those who make malicious, frivolous or vexation complaints?

- Does the employer ensure prompt action when workplace bullying occurs?

- Does the employer provide a clear procedure for making a complaint?

- Does the employer give details of counselling and support services available for the victim?

- Does the employer promise to maintain confidentiality?

The policy should be readily available to all employees.

> **Tip**
>
> It is in the employer's interests to stamp out bullying because its consequences can lead to poor productivity, absenteeism and high staff turnover.

Some estimates put the cost of workforce bullying, in the UK, upwards of £2 billion a year.

What should you do if you are bullied – electronically or face to face

The simple solution is to confront the bully and ask them to stop. This is not always possible and will depend on the circumstances. However, bullies are often cowards. They will find courage in their friends so better to approach the bully privately and say:

> '*I know all about the emails and comments on Facebook that you have been making about me. I'm sure you intended it as a "bit of fun" but frankly, it's gone too far. I have a record of pretty well everything you have written, posted and said. You either stop it now, or I will take whatever action is open to me to make you stop. That includes escalating it to management, the HR department, my trade union rep or the police. It stops, right here, right now. Do you understand?'*

It's tough to do and may not be appropriate in all cases but remember, bullies are cowards, and they can seldom cope with face-to-face confrontation. The important thing is, you carry out whatever you promised to do. If you don't, it will be seen as a sign of weakness and the bully will have won.

Remember to:

- Keep a detailed record of events recording incidents, emails, new posts and Tweets, including date, time, location, what was said or done and names of any witnesses willing to support you.

- Get some support from a friend or a trade union representative.

- Focus on regaining control of the situation by taking positive action in response to the bullying. If you can, confront the bully and carry out your promise to act.

- Is there a workplace bullying policy? Read it and follow it.

- Bring the bullying behaviour to the attention of management as soon as it starts. Don't wait.

- Submit a formal grievance.

Bulling is bullying no matter if it is on the internet or in the office. Take prompt action, don't delay.

Ten tips to prevent online bullying on Facebook

1 *Check your settings* and only let your real friends see your account and message and 'talk' with you. Only people who can access you can bully you. Only allow someone you want as a friend, to be your friend. You can't be friends with someone you don't know or don't trust. If you are approached and you are not sure, say, *'Oh, I'm sorry, I just don't have time for more than the friends I have now and with family members I can't manage any more. But, it was really nice of you to ask.'*

2 *Set up a limited profile* so that you can control how much people, other than your accepted friends, are able to see. Remember, a small amount of information about your movements or interests can become a huge clue to a potential bully.

> **Tip**
>
> Go to the 'Privacy' tab in the Settings and customize the 'Who can see my stuff' section. Be very cautious about which settings you allow to be viewable; keep most things to confirmed friends only – list their names in the limited profiles box.

3 *Learn how to block friends* who don't behave like friends. If someone shows signs of being difficult or unpleasant, don't delay, block them immediately.

> **Tip**
>
> Go to Settings and click on the 'Blocking' tab. There you will see a 'Block users' section. Type in the name or email of the person you'd like to block. Facebook will warn you that once you have blocked a person they cannot be your friend on Facebook and won't be able to interact with you (except through applications and games you both use). Click on the 'Block' button.

4 *Learn to spot bullying tactics.* Online conversations and comments can easily hide a person's real intentions. Sometimes it is hard to spot and it is just as easy to misinterpret an innocent remark. The following could be indications of someone trying to bully you:

- Wall posts that say intimidating, unkind, or nasty things about you, your friends, and the things you care about.

- Consistent abuse about the things you've posted. For example: 'Why do you post such STUPID things???? You're a waste of space!!!!'

- The use of lots of punctuation, such as WTF?!!! on a consistent basis, intended to ram home a message without any subtlety.

- The use of ALL CAPITALS can denote a menacing attitude.

> **Tip**
>
> Online etiquette views most usage of ALL CAPITALS as the
> equivalent of shouting and, if the message is accompanied by
> negative words or implications, assume it is an attempt to intimidate.

- Posting photos or videos of you online that are uncom-
  plimentary, or tagging you in photos that suggest negative
  things, might be a clue to what is to come.
- The use of threatening, harassing or bad language in Facebook
  chat.
- Someone starting a Facebook group based on you, such as
  something like '10 reasons to hate Janet B', 'Why Ian is a
  useless manager'.

5 *Look for a pattern.* Be sure that anything that upsets you is not
just a one-off stupid, petty or insulting comment that was added
thoughtlessly. It might just be careless. If it happens again
assume it is deliberate. Does it reflect how the person reacts to
you in real life? Is this something they're carrying over from
their everyday behaviour?

It is possible for just one thing to be enough to establish
harassing behaviour, such as threatening you, or adding
compromising photos of you with suggestive comments, etc.

6 *Tell the bully to stop.* It might be enough to ask the person to
stop bothering you. Message them quietly at first. If they keep it
up, leave a public request; knowing that your other friends can
read it might shame them into ceasing. Bullies are usually
cowards and back off when challenged.

If the bully is someone known to you in a professional
capacity, remind them they need to remain professional when
they are online. Remind them your wall is read by a lot of people
who will form a view of them as well as you! If they post
unpleasant comments other people will see them.

7 *Talk to your close friends about what is happening.* They may be able to leave messages asking the bully to stop as well, and to make it obvious in public that the bully's behaviour is unwanted and not tolerated.

8 *Don't stoop to play their game.* You might feel safer responding in kind from the relative 'safety' of your computer, but this will only increase the problem, and could end in a real-life confrontation. Don't delay, just block a bully.

9 *Report them.* There's no need to pussyfoot around if you've been nice and things didn't stop. Report the behaviour that is upsetting you. Contact the Facebook administrators; keep records and screenshots, outline the facts and the impact that the bullying is having on you and request they take action. Say you want the offensive material removed. For more information, see Facebook's own instructions at: http://www.facebook.com/help/.

The police should be involved if you have received physical threats, racial taunts, or if photos or videos of you are being changed in Photoshop to give a false impression.

10 *Close your Facebook account.* If you're really unhappy using the Facebook account and things feel out of control, or you feel over-exposed, consider deleting it. You can always open a new account later.

Remember, you can always open a new Facebook account using a different name, such as your first and middle name. You may need to talk to Facebook administrators about opening an account with a 'non-real' name but if bullying is the issue, then you have good grounds for being exempted from the usual name policy.

> **Tip**
>
> Be prepared to wait for Facebook to erase the pages. You might have to wait a while: they are not known for being prompt.

One final thought: what do you want a Facebook page for? LinkedIn could be a better option for managers and people in business.

Summary points

- New technologies mean that traditional bullies are able to hide behind the anonymity of a computer screen and operate as cowards that can be difficult to stop.

- Limit your vulnerability to cyberbullying by being very selective of what you post online. You should also keep records of everything and seek support from others if attacked by a cyberbully.

- If it comes to it, involve management, your trade union or the police, but don't back down.

20

If things don't change they'll stay the same

There are four Cs in change

Do you remember the early 1990s management buzz-phrase 'change management'? I've never really understood the meaning of that expression. What is the purpose of management if it is not to see through change? Change is at the very heart of management.

Indeed, some of the managers I come across are little more than process managers. The test of real managers is their ability to manage change. It takes leadership, courage and an understanding of what makes people tick. Why do people hate change? Here are the answers. There are four Cs in change:

Table 20.1 The 4 Cs

Cross	Cross that things are changing
Confused	Confused about what is happening
Cast-off	Cast-off, feeling left behind or being unwanted
Chaos	Chaos, in the sense that disaffected people will look for another job, good people will jump ship (while they know they can) and the rest will work in a battlefield of smouldering resentment that makes it impossible to see what's happening.

The four Cs are not phases we all go through, and the passage from one to the other is not necessarily a pathway that everyone will follow. But you can bet that all of us will go through some of them and some of us will go through all of them.

> ## Tip
>
> Understanding the four Cs in change is at the heart of what you need to know about managing change. They are the fundamentals.

They are the emotional responses through which people will go. The workplace has changed a great deal and no one expects a job for life. We all work where we work for a variety of reasons. The reasons span from 'the only place I can get a job', through to 'I love the work and the people I work with'. They can be 'I'm using this job as a stepping stone to a better job', right across the spectrum to 'I'm marking time till I retire'.

You could list a thousand different reasons why a thousand different people work where they do. What do they have in common? With very rare exceptions, people all work because they have to. They need the money. In other words, they need the security. Change threatens security. It's as simple as that. If working people don't feel secure, they worry, they become difficult and their performance drops.

Dealing with difficult people through a period of change

The first thing is to expect people to be difficult! Even the ones who are usually a delight to work with – expect the worse! Remember, it's the security thing. Security (or the lack of it) eats into the nice people along with the not-so-nice people.

> **Tip**
>
> It is seldom the case that everything has to be changed. The trick of the great change-masters is to recognize the past and take the best of it into the future. Let's look at the four Cs in more detail.

Cross

Cross? Of course, wouldn't you be? You've been a loyal employee in a job for ages. You've done your best and given everything that has been asked of you. Suddenly someone wants to change everything around. You'll go home and moan to your family, you'll moan to your friends and you'll moan to the people you work with.

What's the answer? Easy. Ask *'Christopher, I know you're cross about the changes that are taking place. Tell my why and let's see if there is anything we can do'*: a few simple words designed to get the conversation focused. Expect 'Don't ask me. No one ever listens to me.' Come back with, *'I'm sorry you feel that way. I'm listening now. What do you think I should know?'* Ask people what was good about their job before the change.

Don't raise expectations and do be realistic. However, you can be sympathetic and you can be understanding and supportive. *'I know change is difficult for us all, but if we don't move to a more up-to-date working practice, our overheads will continue to rise and that affects our competitiveness.'* Or, *'I know how much you've put into your work and that is the reason we'd like you to try doing it another way. Who better to give it a real try for a couple of months and be able to evaluate it against some solid experience?'* Agree a course of action that involves poor old Christopher the Cross.

Confused

If you've been doing the same job for years, probably in the same way, you'll be confused when someone comes along and changes everything. It's more than the 'job thing'. This time it is more about self-image and a feeling of loss. This is a common feeling among employees who have been with the organization for a long time. Change can give them a genuine feeling of loss.

They will be wondering how (or even if) they fit in. Highlight the changes and how they can lead to a lot more job satisfaction. Say, *'Colin, you've done a great job for us and we hope that the changes will make the job easier/faster/quieter/safer/more satisfying/give you more [or less] customer contact.'* Concentrate on the positive side of the changes and how they translate into a benefit for Confused Colin.

Cast-off

Of all of the four Cs, this one has to be the most common. There is another C lurking behind this: communication, that 13-lettered word again, unlucky for some. The bigger the company, the more complex the change, the faster it is introduced, the more people will not have a clue what is going on.

This one needs all of your patience. You may well have sent out 27 tonnes of inter-company newsletters, held goodness knows how many briefing sessions and bombarded the organization with helpful emails. There will still be one or two (or more often more) individuals who still don't know what's going on.

Listen to people's views on their new department, or workplace, or job. You'll hear them say, 'There's no place for an older person like me any more.' Explain how they fit into the new organization, the reasons for change and the part they can play:

'Catherine, I'm sorry if all this change has made you feel we don't value you. That is really not the case. The important

thing is the new company needs to have experienced people like you around, we need your know-how to help us develop into the future. Now, tell me, what are you not sure about?'

Now here's the trick. Don't leave it there. People who claim to be confused and to not know what is going on sometimes use it as a defence mechanism. In other words, they don't want to know what is going on. So agree some objectives that are related to the change and monitor the outcomes. That way the 'confused' become engaged.

Give Catherine the Cast-off a place to hide and often she will!

Tip

Small companies have communication gaps, too. Bosses often think that because it is a small company everyone knows what's going on – not true. Small companies have to communicate too!

Two tricks in managing change: spell it out, and interest people. Spell out the changes as often and as clearly as you can. Be prepared to clarify again and again.

Second, do it in a way that interests people. Explain the changes, not from the corporate point of view (that needs to be done, but not now), but from how it will affect the individual, what it means to them, personally, day to day. This engages people in the change process on a personal level.

Chaos

'I have no idea where I fit into this mess. I don't know what I'm supposed to be doing. All I know is, this is a mess.' You're bound to hear that sometime from someone.

Start with a confidence builder. Ask Charlie to spell out what he thinks the changes are, then say, *'Well, that's a pretty good summary. Let's take a moment and look at the detail.'* No matter what he's said, it's time to start at the beginning and get Charlie the Chaotic back on track. It's better than saying, *'Charlie, even a complete idiot could understand this. What's up with you?'*

When does management become manipulation? The really great managers maintain the self-confidence and balance of those around them. They encourage staff to believe in themselves, and find ways of showing staff they believe in them.

Exercise

Reflect on a time when you have experienced change. Can you relate to the feelings outlined in the 4Cs? How did you feel and could the situation have been handled better by those around you? How?

Summary points

- Change has the potential to unsettle many people and make them difficult to deal with because it threatens the security of their jobs and their very being.

- People will often be cross about change. Ask them to explain their reasoning and see if there's anything you can do to alleviate their concerns.

- Change will also cause a lot of confusion and self-doubt in people; reassure them and explain where they stand in relation to the changes happening.

- People will often feel cast off in periods of change and this has to do with a lack of communication. Make sure they are kept informed and engaged in the change effort and don't let them feel left out.

- If people feel like the situation is chaotic and they don't know how they fit in with the change, go through things in detail with them.

21
A fast-track guide to conflict and how to handle it

What conflict is

The precise definition of 'conflict' is: a direct disagreement of ideas or interests, a battle or struggle, antagonism or opposition. Add to that incompatibility and interference and you get a pretty ugly picture.

However it is defined, you'll know it when you've got it. What's involved, or in guru speak, what are the dynamics of conflict?

There are two fundamentals at work:

- the objective differences between the participants;
- the emotions and perceptions that come as the gift wrapping.

People react to conflict in five basic ways: two Ps and three Cs:

1 Put it off: they will avoid it, pretend it doesn't exist and put off having to deal with it.

2 Put up with it: generally resulting in letting someone get their own way.

3 Compromise: they'll look for a win–win where both (or all) sides give up something to reach an agreed conclusion.

4 Carry on fighting: when one, both or all sides are not prepared to give ground and they carry on slugging it out until they drop!

5 Collaborate: when a mutually agreed solution is arrived at and everyone has their needs addressed. Not necessarily met – but addressed.

Number 5, collaborating, is ideal – but it is the hardest to achieve. It needs two more Ps, patience and persistence – with a few gallons of perspiration! It is important to recognize both elements of conflict. You can't deal with the differences in a clinical way without considering the emotions involved.

Tip

Be clear, conflict will not be effectively resolved if there is no facility for emotional release in conflict resolution.

Dealing with conflict: 10 steps to cooling it

What can you do about conflict? Is conflict inevitable? No, it is not. Here are 10 simple steps to take to defuse the situation, take the sting out of the issue. You can be the one who takes it all in their stride, and you can be the one to be cool under fire. You can be the peacemaker and you don't have to be the living incarnation of Mother Teresa to do it. It's simple, really.

Table 21.1   Ten steps to defusing a situation

Step 1 Manage aggression face to face	Not by email, text or phone. Peace makers 'do it face to face'. Difficult? Sometimes, yes it is. But leaving messages and sending billets-doux just creates a compost in which resentment, grudges, rancour, spite and hostility will grow.
Step 2 Demonstrate you understand	Use the phrase 'I understand', but use it with care. Saying 'I understand' can appear supportive and knowing. It also invites the response, 'What do you mean, "you understand"? How could you possibly know?' Better to use the concept of understanding, but in a different way. Try, 'I can see you're very upset. Some time ago I had a big bust-up with someone and was furious and I guess you're feeling the same way. If you are feeling like I was, then I think I understand how you must be feeling.' Saying 'I understand' implies a superior knowledge or being patronizing, and that is likely to make the situation worse. Showing you have an insight into how cross or upset someone is helps to defuse it.
Step 3 Resist the urge to walk away from conflict	Especially if you are feeling threatened. Although, do try to leave before that might happen! If you do feel threatened by what someone is saying to you, resist the temptation to put the shutters up and become non-communicative. You won't resolve the situation by freezing it. Try to keep lines of communication open.

Table 21.1 *continued*

Step 4 Don't become angry	Focus on the issue that has ignited all this ire and find a question to ask. So, when a colleague lets you down with a deadline, 'Dick, could I ask you to get that work onto my desk by tomorrow morning, please?' Why make a request? Step one, thinking of the right request to make provides a nanosecond for you to put the matches away and forget about lighting the fuse. Second, it stops you turning an issue into a wider conflict.
Step 5 Become a mirror, or a tape recorder	If someone is sounding off in an aggressive, threatening way, repeat the exact words they have used to upset you. Play them back exactly as they have used them. 'So, Maureen, you're saying...' (then repeat it back). The chances are, when the person has heard what they have said, they will see how inappropriate or hurtful it is and calm down. Sometimes you have to repeat the words more than once. This technique keeps the focus on one issue and prevents the conversation from throwing itself off an irredeemable height. In management guru speak, it's called centring and keeps the issue in narrow focus.

Table 21.1   *continued*

Step 6 Accept responsibility for your emotions	Don't try and shift the responsibility for your emotions to someone else. It's your anger, so you be accountable for it. Try to say, 'Peter, I feel very cross when you deliver projects to me late and don't warn me that you are running behind schedule.' That's much better than, 'You make me furious when you're late with stuff!' Spot the difference? There's no transference of blame, and it leaves Peter only to explain his lateness and not have to deal with your anger as well. Subtle, but it works – really, or your money back!
Step 7 Picture yourself on the other side of the conflict	If you are trying to manage a conflict, picture yourself putting each side of the argument into the scales. Become like a judge, summing up a court case. Be fair to both sides: 'On the one hand I do see that engineering couldn't have delivered the project on time because sales had not given them the customer's drawings. On the other hand, engineering knew the job was needed in eight weeks and should have asked for the information they needed. However, sales could have been more aware of how non-delivery would jeopardize the whole project. I guess everyone carries their share of the blame. What do we need to do to put it right and make sure it doesn't happen again?'

Table 21.1   *continued*

Step 8 Control your emotions	Take pride in controlling your temper. Get a tight grip on self-control, hold on to your coolness. The more you practise being calm, the better you will get at it. When conflict stares you in the face, say to yourself, this is an opportunity for me to be self-controlled, calm and relaxed. The more you do it, the better you'll be at it. Promise – or your money back!
Step 9 Take a pause	Do nothing. If you know you are about to turn into an Exocet missile, keep off the trigger. Put some time between you, the others and the incident. If someone has jeopardized everything you've been working for, concentrate on what has to be done to salvage it. Letting someone know how you feel might make you feel better but won't sort the problem. Putting some time and distance between you and the 'person who caused all this grief' will take the intensity out of the emotion, and you'll be better able to establish the truth and get to the bottom of the foul-up.
Step 10 Give yourself permission to feel emotional	Do it with dignity. No slamming doors, no table-thumping. It frightens people, others will laugh at you and most important of all, everyone will remember the day you lost control. You'll be remembered for it. You'll be perceived as unpredictable, and that is a step away from unreliable. Going to lose your cool? Do it with decorum and choose your words with care. Be remembered for being smart, not a smasher-upper!

Exercise

Think of the last time you experienced conflict. Which of the 10 steps outlined did you manage? Looking back, how could you have taken any of the steps that you missed? Would it have made a difference? If so, how?

Summary points

- Conflicts are made up of the differences in opinions people might have, as well as of the emotional and perceptual differences that come with that.
- Emotions will muddle up the process but are inherently linked to the conflict, so you need to address them first and foremost.
- Always manage aggression face to face.
- Show you sympathize and try and understand the other person's point of view.
- Always try to resolve things but don't let it get physical.
- Ask people to remedy things first.
- Repeat what people say to you so they can see first-hand how they are coming across.
- Accept and acknowledge how you feel – communicate this to others as well.
- Try and see both sides of the argument.
- Practise at keeping your emotions in check.
- Take a breather if you feel you won't be able to contain the conflict.
- If you're going to get cross, choose your words carefully and don't go overboard.

22
And, finally, finally...

If all this talk of difficult people is depressing you, think of the people who make you happy, the folks who delight you, the ones who you look forward to seeing and who light up your life. The colleagues who are a pleasure to work with and the associates who are reliable, honest, open and fun.

How to deal with *them*? As the universe, galaxy, world, continent, country, county, town and where you work make more and more use of technology to manage their information and messaging, it is easy to forget one of the greatest motivation tools of all. It is simple and becoming an endangered species. It is being eclipsed by email, messaging, texting and data transmission. The elements of the simple and best tool are probably on your desk, right now. They are pen and paper. Never overlook the power of the handwritten note. A thank you card, a note to say well done, can have a huge impact. Use a handwritten note to highlight how well someone has done.

Drop a note to colleagues: *'I've sent a note to Mary to say how well I thought she handled that tricky situation with the Oxford account. Don't you think she did a great job?'*

Write to your boss (why not): *'Thank you for helping me through a difficult time, I really appreciate it.'*

Drop a note to your clients and customers: '*I wanted you to know how much we appreciate the chance to take care of your supply-chain needs. We'll do our very best to give you great service.*'

... and, really finally:

Thank you for buying this book. I hope it is useful for you!

RL

HOW TO MOTIVATE THE SALES TEAM

I once had the job of 'motivating the sales team'. It was a nightmare task to think up new ways of bribing them to perform better! They were a talented lot. Bright and no push-over. They enjoyed success, high incomes. Finding tricks to turn up performance got harder and harder.

One day, while ploughing my way through sales reports and numbers, I had a thought. On average the sales team would prospect 20 leads, make five solid appointments and close two sales. This meant we needed to get 18 people to say 'no' to get to the two that would say 'yes'.

I turned the whole reporting and reward system on its head. We encouraged people to get the 'noes'. That way, the more 'noes' we got, the closer we were to the next 'yes'. There was an interesting spin-off. The more fuss we made about 'no', the more interested the sales team became in talking about why prospects said 'no'. There was no longer any professional shame and nothing to hide about getting a 'no'.

Techniques were analysed, sales presentation retuned and the product offering refined. It really worked, and the prospect to close ratio doubled as we shared our failures as well as our successes.

REFERENCES

Bramson, R M (1988) *Coping with Difficult People*, Anchor Press/ Doubleday, Garden City, NY

Croner (no date) *CCH Employment Law Manual*, Croner

Keating, C J (1984) *Dealing with Difficult People*, Paulist Press, Ramsey, NJ

Keyton, J (1999) Analysing interaction patterns in dysfunctional teams, *Small Group Research*, 20(4) (August), pp 491–503

Lewis-Ford, B K (1993) Management techniques: coping with difficult people, *Nursing Management*, 24(3) (March), pp 36–38

McRae, B (1998) *Negotiating and Influencing Skills: The art of creating and claiming value*, Sage, Thousand Oaks, CA

Peters, T J and Waterman, R H (1982) *In Search of Excellence*, Harper and Row, New York

Raffenstein, M (2000) Dealing with difficult people on the job, *Current Health 2*, 26(5) (January), pp 16–22

Rosner, B (2000) Surviving sceptics, dealing with Doubting Thomases at work, *ABC News*, March (available online from: www.abcnews.go.com/business)

Webster's (1995) *Webster's II New Riverside Dictionary*, Houghton Mifflin, Springfield, MA

FURTHER READING

Arnot Ogden Medical Centre (no date) Self care: difficult people (available online from: www.aomc.org/Hod2/general/stress-Difficult.html)

Axelrod, A and Holtje, J (1997) *201 Ways to Deal with Difficult People*, McGraw-Hill, New York, NY

Cole, L L (1995) Dealing with difficult people, *Executive Excellence*, **12**(1) (January)

Executive Edge (1996) How to handle difficult people (available online from: www.smartbiz.com/sps/arts/exe104.html)

Kottler, J A (1994) Working with difficult group members, *Journal for Specialists in Group Work*, **19**(1) (March), pp 3–8

Landolt, S and Hochgraf, L (1997) Dealing with difficult people, *Credit Union Management*, (November)

Sammy's place (no date) Six types of difficult people at work and how to avoid conflict with each (available online from: http://members.aol.com/spers62774/six.html)

Solomon, N (1990) *Working with Difficult People*, Prentice-Hall, Englewood Cliffs, NJ

Strom-Gottfried, K (1998) Applying a conflict resolution framework to disputes in managed care, *Social Work*, **43**(5) (September)